Uncontair

Incitements

Visit the series web page at: edinburghuniversitypress.com/series/incite

Uncontainable Legacies

Theses on Intellectual, Cultural, and Political Inheritance

Gerhard Richter

EDINBURGH
University Press

Edinburgh University Press is one of the leading university presses in the UK. We publish academic books and journals in our selected subject areas across the humanities and social sciences, combining cutting-edge scholarship with high editorial and production values to produce academic works of lasting importance. For more information visit our website: edinburghuniversitypress.com

Edinburgh University Press Ltd
The Tun – Holyrood Road, 12(2f) Jackson's Entry, Edinburgh EH8 8PJ

Typeset in Bembo
by R. J. Footring Ltd, Derby, UK, and
printed and bound in Great Britain

A CIP record for this book is available from the British Library

ISBN 978 1 4744 8780 1 (hardback)
ISBN 978 1 4744 8782 5 (webready PDF)
ISBN 978 1 4744 8781 8 (paperback)
ISBN 978 1 4744 8783 2 (epub)

Contents

vii

"It is dangerous to be an heir."
Nietzsche, *Thus Spoke Zarathustra*

1

The One Who Inherits, Interprets.—The one who inherits, interprets. One can even go one step further and aver: The inheritor stands before an enigma that, like an especially refractory text, resists the assignment of meaning. The heir who inherits an intellectual, cultural, or political legacy in the emphatic sense, that is, the heir who opens up to the moment of a radical inheriting, will not cease to interpret, and every true interpretation, for its part, is inseparable from the concept and experience of inheriting—an interpretive questioning of the perpetually shifting meaning of what is handed down.

2

Thetic Inheritance.—To write about inheritance in the form of theses is itself an act of inheritance. One might say that to advance a thesis—the Greek θέσις—names the act of putting forth a proposition, the setting-forth of a textual artifact which then becomes a potential object of intellectual inheritance. Or, to phrase it in a manner more closely informed by the original Greek: A thesis is a position one can stand on. In this sense, one advances *to* a thesis, as a thesis already inheres. It is not a completely new invention but presupposes something that already exists, a kind of inheritance. Seen from this perspective, a thesis simultaneously figures as a potential object of inheritance and presupposes inheritance. Indeed, the very idea and practice of writing in the thetic form must first be inherited from an elsewhere, an unruly and heterogeneous legacy that includes such texts as Aristotle's *De Interpretatione*, Luther's *Ninety-Five Theses*, Marx's "Theses on Feuerbach," Gershom Scholem's "95 Theses on Judaism," and Walter Benjamin's theses "On the Concept of History," among many others. There can be no thesis without inheritance and no theses *on* inheritance without the inheritance *of* theses.

3

Ideal Reader. — The ideal reader of these theses on inheritance does not yet exist — that is, before the theses and in advance of their particular arguments. This reader is still to be formed, even created, by an encounter with them, inheriting the theses, if he or she is able and willing, in a singular and as-yet unpredictable way. Themselves objects of inheritance even as they thematize this trope, the theses await interpretation on the part of the reader. One might even venture to say that the ideal reader-inheritor of these theses on inheritance will be someone who does not merely inhabit the world in any single mode, in any particular time and place alone. This refusal to identify fully with a supposedly contemporaneous world holds open the possibility of a certain reflective engagement with what is encountered in that world, including these theses on inheritance. As the young Nietzsche puts it in 1872 in the introduction to a book he never completed on the future of our educational institutions and their inherited legacies: "We do not envy the people who feel completely at home in the present and consider contemporary conditions 'self-evident' — neither for this belief of theirs nor for this scandalously intellectual term 'self-evident,' so in vogue nowadays." On the contrary, those who are most fully able to receive these reflections on intellectual inheritance most likely find themselves strangely out of joint with their "own" times and their contemporary life-world. To them, very little appears self-evident. This is not to say that they are simply old-fashioned or nostalgic about some prelapsarian state or condition; their restless vigilance, however, will not allow them to take any kind of contemporaneity — and least of all their own — for granted.

In the preface to that same unfinished book (and separate from its introduction), Nietzsche expresses his hope for a reader of the kind the present theses on inheritance desire: "The reader I hope for must have three qualities: He must read calmly, without haste; he mustn't always let himself and his 'culture' intrude into his reading; and finally, he must not expect a concrete result, some tables and charts at the end. . . . The present book will never satisfy the chart lovers." To read unhurriedly; to bracket, as far as possible, the ideological preconceptions of one's time; and to renounce the expectation that the arguments circulating through the theses can be reduced to a merely instrumental form—these are virtues conducive to a way of inheriting that is receptive to the potentiality these theses might harbor.

4

No Conservatism.—An intellectual inheritance is not to be equated with a nostalgic tending of tradition, whereby this or that imagined community passes on its cultural capital with the aim of preserving an identity whose meaning remains stable and unaffected by the act of transmission.

5

Triple Temporalities.—To inherit something means both to acquire it and, in turn, to relay it to others. The temporality of inheriting thus always unfolds along a triple axis. The heir receives something in the *present* from a *past* that, in turn, will be the object of a *future* act. An engagement with inheritance thus inscribes the heir forcefully in the human experience of time as such. It is hardly an accident that Augustine writes in *Contra Julianum*, "quod a patribus acceperunt, hoc filiis tradiderunt," which can be rendered in English as "what they have received from their fathers, they transmitted to their sons." An abiding awareness of the multiple temporalities of inheriting necessarily suffuses any emphatic confrontation with an intellectual legacy.

6

Generations. — To learn is to receive an inheritance from an other, a bequest that the heir receives along with the injunction to pass it on to other others. This double other-directedness inherent in the act of inheriting embodies a significant part of what is to be learned from inheritance as such. In an address to school children on the topic of teachers and pupils, later included in his 1933 collection of writings entitled *Mein Weltbild* (translated in 1934 as *The World As I See It*), Albert Einstein remarks: "Bear in mind that the wonderful things you learn in your schools are the work of many generations. All this is put in your hands as your inheritance in order that you may receive it, honor it, add to it, and one day faithfully hand it on to your children." To learn to read, think, and write is to learn how to hand down what has been handed down.

The Difficulty of Using Freely What Is One's Own.—The
thinking of inheritance opens onto the difficult task of learning
to relate to what is supposedly one's own in a free and uncir-
cumscribed manner. In order to appreciate this thought, it is
helpful to recall how modern German literature commences, in
its most canonical text, paradigmatically with a reflection upon
the difficult question of inheriting: At night, in his Gothic study,
Goethe's Faust not only considers the relative advantages and
disadvantages of science and scholarship for one's understanding
of human life, but he also explicitly includes among the most
urgent questions of one's being-in-the-world the problem of
inheritance. In a multilayered soliloquy, Faust says: "What you
have inherited from your fathers, / Acquire it to gain possession
of it" ("Was Du ererbt von deinen Vätern hast, / Erwirb es, um
es zu besitzen"). Goethe is not merely concerned, in an alle-
gorical mode, with problems of aesthetics, such as the question
concerning modern appropriations of the classical Greek
heritage or the dramatic legacy of Shakespeare, which often
claim his attention. After all, according to Faust's statement,
what has been inherited—and thus presumably already trans-
ferred to the property of another—does not simply *belong* to
that other without further reflection. What has been inherited
first demands to be acquired not only in the juridical, economic,
or material senses. The inheritance demands to be inherited *as*
inheritance. In other words, a proper inheritance requires that
one learn how to inherit *as such.*

Goethe's contemporary Hölderlin thinks in a similar vein.
In a letter to Böhlendorf from December 4, 1801, Hölderlin

wonders to what extent modernity must become heir to the refractory heritage of Ancient Greece in order to recognize what is its own—yet without ever being able to understand that heritage fully. In so doing, Hölderlin raises a principal problem concerning inheritance, that is, the question as to whether what one considers one's own must first be negotiated in relation to the gift (or curse) of what has been inherited and, by extension, in relation to what has long passed and become an object of transmission. "But what is one's own," he writes in relation to the experience of what has been inherited, "must be learned fully as well as what is foreign" ("Aber das Eigene, muß so gut gelernt seyn, wie das Fremde"), to the extent that "the *free* use of *what is one's own* is the most difficult" ("der *freie* Gebrauch des Eigenen das schwerste ist"). Only through what is other, foreign, or strange—*das Fremde*—does that which is one's own—*das Eigene*—become visible as what it always already was: something that is one's own but that lives only in and through the foreign. In other words, *das Eigene* can only come into its own through the foreignness that silently already inhabits it. After all, a substantive act of inheriting posits, as both Hölderlin and Goethe make vivid, that the actual act of inheriting is still to come, while this positing itself is able to occur only on the basis of an inheritance that already has come to pass.

Elusive Inheritance. — In the case of an inheritance — especially an intellectual one — the heir can be certain of neither the content nor the structure of the legacy to be received. When the rigorous interpretation of the inheritance is still to be accomplished, the object of that inheritance may well resist its transfer into the presumed property of the heir. After all, one cannot speak of a new property in the moment of its inheritance because the inheritance, even if it appears more or less transparent, always also demands to be *inherited in another way*: by means of a slow, groping, hesitant interpretation. Without the gradual and incremental learning-to-understand that always is preceded by a certain consternation and helplessness, the inheritance becomes, as Faust fears, a worrisome burden, a form of uselessness, an enigma that weighs down the heir. What exactly is it, then, that Faust must learn? Apparently, the disciplines of philosophy, law, medicine, and theology, in which he already has distinguished himself, are not of any help to him as his quest and questioning unfold. Rather, what Faust must learn is the task of inheriting itself, the inheritance of inheritance *as* inheritance.

9

Inheriting a Feeling.—In order to receive an inheritance at all, an heir must encounter what comes from another with a certain open resourcefulness that could not have been rehearsed in advance of any singular act of inheriting. This is the sense in which Freud interprets the lines on inheritance in *Faust*, which were among his favorite passages in Goethe. In *Totem and Taboo*, for instance, he reflects upon the ways in which "the psychical continuity in the sequence of generations" deserves our attention. Freud adds—by inheriting from Goethe without naming him explicitly—that a "part of the problem seems to be met by the inheritance of psychical dispositions which, however, need to be given some sort of impetus in the life of the individual before they can be roused into actual operation. This may be the meaning of the poet's words: 'Was Du ererbt von deinen Vätern hast, / Erwirb es, um es zu besitzen.'" What Freud in the same vein calls a *Gefühlserbschaft*, an inherited feeling or a heritage of emotion, thus finds its condition of possibility precisely in the disclosive experiential interaction of what has been inherited and what is one's own. In the peculiar form of a *Gefühlserbschaft*, inheritance works to transmit even emotions that are based on experiences that one did not have—and typically could not have had—oneself. For instance, the children or even grandchildren of victims of psychological traumatization can still be decisively affected by the transmitted trauma and its inherited feeling. The children and grandchildren of genocide survivors can display emotions that are, while inflected by their own singular experience, also heavily indebted to the traumatic experience of those who came before them and who have passed down, even if unconsciously or unwittingly, the heritage of that feeling to one or more subsequent generations. Likewise, the children of survivors of war experiences may evidence a *Gefühlserbschaft*, as may, in turn, their children. In this connection, contemporary psychological research in the German context has coined the terms "Kriegskinder" (children of war) and, more recently, "Kriegsenkel" (grandchildren of war). It appears, in principle, that this genealogy of emotional heritage could be extended even further down the line.

Building on Freudian insights, Nicolas Abraham and Maria Torok have investigated, as a symptom in transgenerational trauma, the idea of the unspeakable secret that hands itself down. In the so-called crypt, a psychological secret entombs a wish that must not be articulated and is not readily accessible but that is powerfully operative, even in the form of a denial, in psychical life. One might say that the crypt, among other things, entombs the psychological inheritance of generations.

To be sure, it is possible to inherit feelings. Yet the abiding difficulties that attend the receiving and understanding of such inherited emotions are no less pronounced than they are in the case of opening up to an intellectual inheritance, a legacy of ideas and thoughts. And in either case, we must first attempt to develop a feeling for the particular inheritance and the singular demands that it makes on us—each time unique, each time unpredictable.

10

Who Is the Human Being?—Whatever else may be said about the human and its particular modes of inhabiting the world, the human and the act of inheriting are fundamentally entwined. Might it even be possible to think the essence of the human being in terms of inheriting? Heidegger, for one, thinks so. For instance, in his reading of Hölderlin's poetry, he pauses to reflect: "Who is the human being? . . . [T]he human being is the heir and the one who learns . . . in all things" ("Wer ist der Mensch? . . . [D]er Mensch [ist] der Erbe und der Lernende . . . in allen Dingen").

11

Homo Hereditans.—In recent years, the critical field has become increasingly attuned to forms of transmission and their variegated movements in intellectual, cultural, historical, political, and biopolitical contexts. Problems of inheritance have come to be examined in light of sociohistorical, legal, economic, sociological, anthropological, religious, and literary considerations, among others. One might say that what unites such heterogeneous impulses is a critical receptivity to the ways in which "traditions, transmissions, and what has been received, along with matters of futurity, become the object of justified worry," such that one should think the "human being as a *homo hereditans*, an heir and a bequeather." By the same token, it is not coincidental that inheriting always has to do with "conferring, transmitting, handing down" and that what is shared by all forms of a transmitting inheritance is that "they create a relation among bequeather, inheritance, and heir." What becomes apparent before this backdrop is that the situations of inheriting "presuppose a ceasura" through which an "interruption in the chain of beings, things, or events"—necessary for the possibility of an inheritance and its transmission—can first come to pass; this transmission unfolds according to certain symbolic rules, regardless of whether it obeys or violates them. The thinking of this multilayered caesura gives rise to a multiplicity of diverse research projects in historical and cultural studies, but also in the social sciences and in the history of law and of medicine, all of which may approach the central problem of inheritance from their particular institutional and disciplinary vantage points. Yet the theses on inheritance assembled here are not meant to provide a comprehensive intellectual history of inheritance or to attempt a classification and cataloguing of various models of inheriting and transmitting in such discourses as the law, literary history, sociology, biopolitics, and political theory. Neither is it the task of the theses to offer a cultural history of inheritance or even a reconstruction of the post-Augustinian constellation of inheritance, sin, and modernity as Peter Sloterdijk recently has attempted it with regard to a kind of secularization of the Original Sin. Instead, the concept and experience of an intellectual inheritance will emerge according to the ways in which they always both require and suspend a certain readability. The problems of inheritance, along with its perpetual reinscriptions in differing contexts, here become visible precisely as conceptual issues of refractory interpretation and of deferred understanding.

12

Ruptured Temporalities. — Inheritance always occurs in ruptured time, which is to say disrupted and realigned time. In the act of inheriting, the heir relates to a legacy that comes from a time in the past, yet the reception of that legacy always occurs in the present. The present of inheriting is at odds with itself to the extent that it orients itself toward that which is not merely present, does not spring from the present, but rather issues forth from a time that is no longer. What is more, the present in which the heir relates to the past is itself directed toward a futurity. After all, one never inherits something from the past in order merely to curate that past as if it were a museum, that is, as if it were of historical interest alone. Rather, one inherits from the past in the present with an eye to a future that is always yet to come, a possible futurity in which what the present receives from the past, however enigmatic, can be put to use in this or that manner — which is also to say: politically. Past, present, and future relate to each other in ever-shifting ways when they jointly inhabit the scene of inheritance. In that sense, the heir experiences a ruptured temporality, in which time itself, as Shakespeare's Hamlet would put it, appears to be out of joint.

13

Language. —Inheritance, if it occurs at all, comes to pass in and as language. The act of inheriting is a linguistic, textual act, even as it opens onto the conceptual.

14

Other Languages, Languages of the Other. — The heir receives the remains that constitute an inheritance like a language that, despite being endowed, as it were, with its own structure and grammar, nevertheless must be effortfully acquired. Actual inheriting takes place in language and is transmitted as language. What is to be inherited is always the other language and the language of the other, a language that does not cease to be different by virtue of our endeavoring to acquire it.

15

We Are What We Inherit. — If we are the ones who inherit — and, indeed, if we are what we inherit — we also are the ones who inherit the means by which they may bear witness to the very fact that they are the ones who inherit and that they are their own inheritance. As Jacques Derrida remarks in "The Deconstruction of Actuality": "What we are, we inherit. And we inherit the language that serves to testify to the fact that we are what we inherit." There can be no language with which to testify to our own inheritance — our being-heir, as it were — that is not itself the object of an inheritance. The language with which we bear witness and testify to our being-heir is always already itself inflected in the most decisive manner by its own status as a legacy that precedes any of its speakers, readers, and writers — and that, by extension, will long outlive them as it becomes the inheritance of future heirs, yet to be born.

16

Saying.—When one says that to inherit is to inherit, one employs a tautology. Better to say: to be is to inherit. Or: to inherit is to be.

17

Always Already.—When heirs come to recognize themselves as heirs, they find themselves, to their astonishment, *already inheriting.*

18

Ghostly Traces. — That which is to be inherited issues the demand for a never-ending hermeneutic engagement with it — its sense, its meaning, and, not least of all, its idiosyncratic patterns of interpretation, its each-time-unique theory of reading. If inheritance is not viewed as a presupposition-less appropriation — as the taking-possession of a content that already has been seen through and understood, merely awaiting its transfer into the sphere of what already exists, and has been thought through, in what is one's own — then the uncanny, even ghostly trace that is inscribed in it may emerge in its full distinctness. One need only recall the cursed inheritance in Nathaniel Hawthorne's novel *The House of the Seven Gables*, with its depiction of a lethal curse on the Pyncheon family, a curse that is visited upon family members whenever they open up to what is evil and wrong. In other words, even the kind of inheritance that was already awaited or expected occurs as something un-expected. This is so to the extent that the inheritance does not communicate merely itself (if it can communicate anything at all) but also the irreducible demand to learn to read it in such a way that this learning-how-to-read itself already figures as the *content* of the inheritance — its reach as well as its challenge to the reflecting and questioning consciousness. At stake may be a material, biological, legal, cultural, or religious inheritance, or, as is the case in the present theses, the politics of an *intellectual* inheritance.

19

Undecidability. — Whether a particular inheritance is to be considered a blessing or a curse tends to remain in the realm of undecidability. The more an heir ponders this question as he or she engages with a refractory legacy, the less he or she is able to decide. It is no coincidence that Hawthorne records the uncanny retreat of an inheritance from transparent decidability in an 1849 notebook entry with great economy: "To inherit a great fortune. To inherit a great misfortune."

20

Question Marks. — An intellectual inheritance is not merely the cognitive counterpart to a handing-down of material assets, a reproduction of the political economy whose dismantling Marx and Engels call for in *The Communist Manifesto* in the form of an "abolition of all right of inheritance" ("Abschaffung des Erbrechts"). Rather, genuine inheriting grasps the tradition that it receives as an irreducible question mark, an unexpected challenge, and an enigmatic provocation.

21

Endings, Beginnings.—A true inheritance commences only *after* something else has come to an end—an end that will have emerged at the same time as something other than itself, namely, as a new beginning. In this case, the absence, departure, or death of the bequeather occasions the beginning of an interpretive engagement and the possibility of a future reinscription. As Ernst Bloch laconically remarks, "Even the death of Christ was only his beginning."

22

Ends of Time. — If an inheritance first becomes an object of thought only in the aftermath of a demise or departure, then the futurity of an heir enters a special relation with the absence of the bequeather. In an early reflection, Walter Benjamin observes: "For immortality is only in dying, and time arises at the end of times" ("Denn Unsterblichkeit ist nur im Sterben und Zeit erhebt sich am Ende der Zeiten"). One way of glossing Benjamin's apodictic statement is to read it from the viewpoint of inheritance. Immortality, understood as a mode of living on, cannot be had in the infinite survival of a life but only following the demise of a life — in its finitude. Only once a life ends, that is, only once it can no longer survive in accordance with its own wishes and principles, does its legacy become inheritable by others, in whose lives it lives on. Particularly in the case of an intellectual legacy — say, the teachings of a Nietzsche or a Kierkegaard — a bequeather must first *pass on* (in the double sense of dying and handing down) before future generations can truly open up to an inheritance, read it closely, interpret it without the direct guidance of the originator, and reinscribe it in necessarily different contexts that could not have been foreseen by the testator. If a certain "immortality" (*Unsterblichkeit*) is implied in the process of handing something down to future generations of interpreting heirs, such immortality is precisely a function of mortality. But this kind of *Unsterblichkeit* is not to be confused with the idea of eternal life in the religious sense, say, of a Christian afterlife. There is no trope of redemption at work here, no salvation. Rather, the time of true inheriting arises when time has come to an end (*am Ende der Zeiten*) and the bequeather has run out of time. The end of time, in such a case, is at once the beginning of time — the moment in which time arises *as* time, which is to say, as the time of an uncontainable inheritance.

23

Life and Death. — Viewed from the vantage point of inheritance, life and death are no longer merely opposites. Rather, they are imbricated with each other. On the one hand, as Rainer Maria Rilke writes, "there is death in life, and it astonishes me that we pretend to ignore this." After all, "we must learn to die. That is all of life." On the other hand, one may add that, when it comes to inheritance, there also is life in death — again, not in the religious sense of an afterlife but rather in the sense of an urgent legacy or perpetual injunction that lives on in the hands of heirs, that is, of others who are still alive. In this way, inheritance disrupts the neat demarcation that separates life and death as polarities of each other.

24

Leave-Taking. — In keeping with its enigmatic character, the act of inheriting takes place under the sign of leave-taking, loss, change, and the mourning that often accompanies it. The legacy of someone who is deceased and now, after already having taken leave, participates, through his or her estate as if with a ghostly hand — possibly by means of a testamentary last will — in guiding the destinies of those who are left behind, tacitly provokes an intensification of that which may have appeared to the heir, already during the time when the testator was still alive and in spite of any possible intimacy with the absent one, as something rather enigmatic, irresolvable, and inexplicable.

25

Orphaned Remains. — An intellectual inheritance reveals itself to the heir neither exclusively nor indisputably as a welcomed enrichment or wished-for gift. Rather than being placed at the heir's disposal in a free and sovereign manner, what imposes itself on consciousness is a responsibility toward the ways in which an inheritance offers itself to interpretation while simultaneously withdrawing from it, but also a certain kind of orphanhood, or a becoming-orphaned. The one who inherits becomes an orphan. This is so not only because an inheritance is typically bequeathed upon the occurrence of a parent's, guardian's, or elder's death, but also because the price that is paid for inheriting something, including an intellectual or immaterial legacy, is to be cast into the condition of having been left behind, a scene of departure and leave-taking, mourning, and the experience of becoming, literally or figuratively, orphaned. There is no inheritance without orphans. Indeed, the primal scene of the *Erbsünde*, which in the Biblical tradition is believed to have set into motion the perpetual sinfulness of humankind into which one is born, is inexorably tied to the scene of Adam and Eve's abandonment, the moment in which they are permanently expelled from the Garden of Eden by their creator.

It is striking to note, therefore, that the etymology of the German word "Erbe" encrypts something of the history of this process of becoming an orphan. The history of the semantically complex word "Erbe" is inseparable from that of the orphan. The origin of the term can be documented in early Germanic and Celtic sources: in Old High German as "erbi" and in Middle High German "erbe," which is genetically related to the Gothic "arbi" and the Old English "ierfi." It is primordially related (the *Duden* etymology speaks of "urverwandt") to the Old Irish "orbe" and the Latin "orbus," meaning "robbed," the Greek "orphanós" (orphaned), and the Armenian "orb" (orphan). These and related formations derive from the Indo-European root "*orbho-" (orphaned; orphan). Therefore, it can be argued that the original meaning of "Erbe" is "orphaned possession" or "possession of the orphan." In the orbit of this same etymological root one finds the ancestors of the German word for "work," that is, "Arbeit," which originally signified the "hard physical labor of an orphaned child," and of the German word for "poor," "arm," which once signified "orphaned." If "Erbe" is always suffused with a form of orphanhood, as the Indo-European "*orbho-" suggests, then an inheritance can always also be thought as a form of becoming orphaned. What is passed on and what is inherited are always also orphaned goods.

But if the orphaned goods of an inheritance are associated with the hard labor of an orphan (the orphan's *Arbeit*), they also evoke the hard, slow, patient, and questioning labor of reading, that is, the laborious process of opening up to receive the language and objects of the other who passes on a legacy. There can be no inheritance in the strong sense of the concept without this labor of orphanhood, without shouldering the burden of a rigorous reading and vigilant reinterpretation. To the extent that "Erben" and "Erbschaft" are etymologically linked to the labor (*Arbeit*) and poverty (*Armut*) of an orphaned child, who emerges as something akin to a serf, the moment of inheritance is touched, in its Sisyphean despair, by a certain mourning. It is no accident that the Old High German "erbi" and the Middle High German "erbe" are not only related to the Anglo-Saxon "erbi" and Middle Low German "erve" but, significantly, also to the Old Norse "erfi," which names a so-called obsequy, a funeral reception or commemoration of the departed. In the latter sense of "erfi," an inheritance always also gathers around death and finitude, the unrepresentable experience of life as death-oriented and resistant to interpretation. The history of language—at least in the German case of the "Erbe"—preserves something of the abiding interpenetration that is not usually visible on the surface but that forever joins an inheritance with a funeral reception, welding the work of mourning, even the hard labor or *Arbeit* of a rigorous textual encounter, with a logic and a language that are seen only in their withdrawal and understood only as distant echoes of a time and a thinking that already are no more.

One of the many precepts that follow from assuming this perspective is that the true heir must learn to recognize herself or himself as an inheritor in mourning who is called upon to engage the difficult labor of learning to read the inheritance. The heir must grasp, in other words, that the inheritance, far from being an appropriable possession, *is* precisely this mournful process of reading and interpreting. As such, the heir is both a child to his or her elders and at the same time—in the moment of recognizing the demands placed upon him or her by the mournful inheritance and its perpetual and properly interminable interpretation—*also* an orphan. According to this logic, we might say that the heir is always already an actual or future orphan, regardless of whether his or her parents are in fact alive or dead. Yet even this perceived orphanhood can never become a matter of mere possession. It can only be thought and shared to the extent that it refuses to be fully possessed, that is, to the extent that it eludes the illusions bestowed upon us by our often premature sense of ownership of this or that experience.

26

Masterless Legacy. — In paragraph 34 of the *Metaphysics of Morals* (1797), Kant expands upon the metaphysical prerequisites of the doctrines of law and of virtue, devoting himself concretely to the question of inheritance. A relentless thinker of inheritance, Kant mobilizes the terms *acquisitio hereditates*, a special kind of transmission (*Übertragung*) between a self and an other, to describe the process of inheriting. Among many other things, Kant is concerned with the idea of avoiding a "res nullis" of inheritance, an inheritance that he calls *herrenlos*, that is, masterless, unclaimed, ownerless, stray, or abandoned. But what if the ownerless, masterless quality of an inheritance always also came to play its part, ranging freely and without guidance or control on the part of a master in a manner that cannot be fully calculated? Yet the fact that the *Herrenlose* lacks a master or owner does not imply that the self that encounters it can be considered a liberated servant or freed subject who, as it were, could now be elevated to the position of his or her own master and owner, that is, to the rank of someone who gives her- or himself her or his own laws (auto-nomia). A masterless or ownerless movement is difficult to contain, as it is inseparable from the laborious demands of interpretation and the restless gestures of wishing to understand.

27

Unwanted Inheritance. — The masterless and ownerless orphan-hood of inheriting denotes not only the fragility of any attempt to ensure a transmission between the bequeather and the heir that is based on a mutual free will in the Kantian sense. Rather, the orphaned quality, even treacherousness, of an inheritance also comes to play a role in those cases in which the bequeather looks to the moment of the inheritance from the standpoint of a certain unfreedom or at least with great reservation. One may recall a passage from Lessing's early comedy fragment "Der Schlaftrunk" ("The sleeping potion"): "To an honest man whose world has soured on him, even the thought of the grave is not as torturous as the thought of a laughing heir." Leaving aside the humorous tone of Lessing's formulation, a rather serious reflection finds expression here. From the perspective of the bequeather, the heir appears as a repulsive figure who attempts to enrich her- or himself in an unbecoming and un-deserved way. The opposite case, too, requires consideration, in which the inheritance fails to deliver to the heir something wanted or desirable but instead appears to the heir only as a monstrous infliction, a haunting imposition, an uncanny visita-tion. Especially with regard to the figurative dimension of an inheritance — its intellectual and historical aspects — a legacy is not always wanted. Already in Ancient Greek depictions of in-heritance, such as Aeschylus's figure of Cassandra in the tragedy *Agamemnon*, inheritance can appear as a curse. Cassandra, the soothsayer, is condemned, along with her offspring, to being neither heard nor believed by the world surrounding her, despite her special visionary abilities. Cassandra possesses, as it were, a pure gaze onto inheritance: each time she realizes her own situation she is brought face to face with the catastrophe of what has come to pass. In contemporary German-language literature, Thomas Bernhard's 1986 novel *Auslöschung. Ein Zerfall* (*Extinction*), the narrator's voice engages—in the course of more than 650 pages of inner monologue that is uninterrupted by paragraphs or breaks—with the problem of an inheritance that is felt to be tragic and unacceptable. Following the sudden death of his parents and his brother in a car accident, the narrator obsessively reflects on the insurmountable difficulties pertaining to an unwanted inheritance. Yet those characters in the novel who believe that the narrator, who appears as a consternated executor of an estate and as a perplexed heir, will submit to the destiny of his cursed inheritance "do not really know me, I told myself, they actually believe that I will accept my inheritance in the way that is required." At the end of the novel, the narrator bequeaths his inheritance to the Israelite Cultural Community of Vienna. One also may consider in this context the heavy burden of inheritance borne by the children of leading Nazi politicians, including the German journalist and author Niklas Frank, whose father, Hans Frank, was sentenced to death at the Nuremberg Trials. The son's book, *Der Vater. Eine Abrechnung* (translated into English as *In the Shadow of the Reich*), confronts his father's crimes against humanity in an unsparingly frank manner. Along similar conceptual lines on the other side of the Atlantic, families in the U.S. have discovered their inscription in the shameful and painful legacy of slavery. For instance, in *Inheriting the Trade: A Northern Family Confronts Its Legacy as the Largest Slave-Trading Dynasty in U.S. History*, Thomas Norman DeWolf and his family reflect in a sustained manner on the agonizing discovery that they descend from the most effective and successful family to profit from the slave trade in U.S. history. They must come to terms with the fact that they are heirs to an especially infamous slave-trading ancestor James DeWolf, a Senator from Rhode Island, who, together with his family, was responsible for forcing over 10,000 human beings from Africa into slavery on the American continent, where he profited to such an extent that, at the time of his death in 1837, he was the second wealthiest individual in the United States. The unpredictable aspects of inheriting an unwanted legacy break forth in such limit-cases with particular force.

28

The Original Unwanted Inheritance. — What is the original unwanted inheritance, the one that weighs with the great heaviness of a curse not only on the immediate heir but on all human heirs to come? It is the *original sin*, which in German, in addition to the terms "Ursünde" ("primordial sin") and "Sündenfall" ("the fall into sin") is most often — and most tellingly — called "Erbsünde" ("inherited sin" or, literally, "inheritance-sin"). The phrase "original sin" emphasizes an originary mistake or aberration, a departure from a previous course or state of affairs, which subsequently led to a fallen, that is, postlapsarian world. Its reference is to the original sin narrated in the Book of Genesis — succumbing to the snake's temptation to eat a fruit from the Tree of Knowledge of Good and Evil in defiance of God's prohibition — which then becomes the primordial sin upon which all subsequent forms of sin are based. Yet the linguistic particularity of the German "Erbsünde" shifts the conceptual emphasis from an originary act itself to the *transmission* and *legacy* of that act. Understood as *Erb-sünde*, the idea of an inheritance-sin ambivalently names *both* the sin that is inherited *and* the sin of inheriting itself, that is, inheritance as sin. *Erbsünde* sets into motion an inheritance that becomes a transmitted legacy, even if — or precisely when — its legacy is poisoned.

From the perspective of the heir and his or her inheritance, one should note that, within the conceptual and theological history of *Erbsünde*, one of the most central debates has focused on the question of culpability and guilt. If the inherited sin can be understood merely as an un-asked-for, unwanted affliction that seizes a subject from elsewhere — another context that always already precedes and therefore in a sense exculpates a guilt-inheriting self—then the question of responsibility and the notion of freedom (in choosing or not choosing to relate to this guilt in a particular way) can hardly be located in any normative realm of individual ethics. For the term *Erbsünde*, which was first introduced into German as an interpretation of the Latin *peccatum originale* by the influential late-medieval German-language preacher Johann Geiler von Kaysersberg and subsequently was firmly established in the German language by Luther, has always fluctuated between an assignment of guilt to the subject and the subject's implicit exoneration owing to its unintentional affliction by something for which it cannot be responsible. There have been thinkers of *Erbsünde*, such as Augustine, who have attempted to mediate the tension between a guilt that can be assumed due to free choice and a guilt that cannot be assumed because the act that caused the original sin stands in a merely derivate relationship to a conscious subject capable of contemplating this guilt. In the wake of the reflections by Augustine and later by Luther, the particular nature of the *Schuld* (which, in German, means both debt and guilt) that is inscribed in *Erbsünde* has continued to occupy thinkers into modernity. The logic and implications of *Erbsünde* have evoked sustained reflections in philosophers as variegated as Kant, Hegel, Kierkegaard, Schleiermacher, and Schopenhauer, among others. The original unwanted inheritance thus provides a topos that is inherited by thinkers and writers across the centuries, as if the inheritance itself were the object of reflection, without which it would be impossible to consider the concepts of heir, legacy, transmission, heritage, and guilt in a rigorous manner.

Unwanted Inheritance, Redux.—There is a particular kind of unwanted inheritance that makes itself felt by means of an unlikely and unexpected reversal. Specifically, an arduous struggle against something—say, an injustice, a destructive behavior, an instance of unnecessary suffering—may ironically and retroactively create a strong bond with precisely what is to be fought and overcome. In such cases, the legacy of the other with which one had wished to part in criticism and rejection is, as it were, inherited in a kind of silent affirmation or adoration. The paradoxical structure of an unwanted, unwitting inheritance can be observed, for instance, by perusing the vast collection of smoking-related memorabilia, cigarette-themed ads, and other collectibles on display in the office of a world-renowned scientist studying the horrendous health effects of smoking. By the same token, it has been said that in order to be a good and effective scholar, even of such a terrible phenomenon as fascism, one must, on some dark and inchoate level of the subconscious, have a special relation to it, "understand" its sinister appeal more than the average person might, and share some of the fascination that it has lamentably exerted in the past. To illustrate this point further, one may recall scenes from a television documentary broadcast many years ago. Its topic was the seemingly ubiquitous infestation of New York City, especially its restaurants and eateries, by cockroaches. The documentary revolved around the life and thought of an especially effective exterminator who was called upon when all other attempts at gaining control over an especially horrendous roach infestation had failed and who went by the name of "Dr. Roach." Like no other, Dr. Roach was able to identify and exterminate even those roach colonies that were unusually well hidden in unexpected spaces, such as deep inside certain walls. When asked how he would explain his unusual gift for locating and exterminating roaches—a talent that surpassed that of all other exterminators—he paused to reflect: "I know what a roach likes and how it thinks and acts. I can think like a roach." His true passion in life was to alleviate even the worst roach infestations; to identify and destroy the pests ruthlessly, even in their most obscure and devious gathering places gave him great pleasure. Yet, in response to the question as to whether it was his goal in life to find and kill all roaches, he answered that if, hypothetically, he were to have the chance to destroy the very last roach, he would not do so. He reported that, after all his years of studying roaches very closely with the aim of killing them most effectively, he had grown quite fond of them. And, in a confession that seemed almost inexplicable even to himself, he shared the fact that, while he killed roaches all day for a living, he also tenderly kept a special few of them in a terrarium in his basement at home, as his pets. It is as if Dr. Roach had inherited, on an intimate and unexpected level, the legacy of the very thing he had set out to destroy. As these examples illustrate, there is a kind of tacit inheritance that imposes itself precisely from the very source that one had wanted to undo. It is not for nothing that Nietzsche observes: "He who fights monsters may wish to see to it that, in the process, he does not become a monster himself" ("Wer mit Ungeheuern kämpft, mag zusehn, dass er nicht dabei zum Ungeheuer wird"). Such can be the unpredictable paradox of a "monstrous" inheritance.

30

Refusals. — The experience of a monstrous inheritance, an inherited curse, or an utterly unwanted bequest invites the question as to the possibility of rejecting or refusing an inheritance. If one brackets certain forms of inheritance such as the biological one — which, after all, typically does not leave a human being any choice, although bio-political factors as well as techniques of genetic manipulation such as "gene editing" increasingly may play a role — the possibility of refusing is always the precondition of accepting. One can only ever accept an inheritance because, in principle, one could also refuse it. Yet if the possibility of a rejection is always already the precondition of its acceptance, one would have to direct one's gaze at the fundamental engagement with an inheritance, the agonistic site of a perpetual struggle, whose outcome will serve as the basis on which to decide between acceptance and rejection.

What would it mean, however, to refuse an inheritance that matters, especially in the intellectual realm? What would the word "refusal" even signify in such a case? After all, in the ongoing interpretive, deliberative engagement with an inheritance, has one not tacitly *already become an heir*? In such a case, it is entirely possible that the one who has engaged — intensively and without reserve — the possibly monstrous aspects of a particular inheritance with the intention to decline it has in actuality already inherited in a much more rigorous sense than the one who believes that he or she may simply "accept" a difficult and weighty inheritance without much intellectual effort and who seeks to arrange him- or herself rather cozily within the space afforded by that inheritance.

31

Hegelian Labors of Inheritance. —Inheriting is hard work. Indeed, an inheritance always involves, if Hegel is to be believed, a form of labor. While Hegel, in the *Phenomenology of Spirit*, speaks of "the labor of the concept" ("Arbeit des Begriffs"), in his later reflections on tradition as they appear in the *Lectures on the History of Philosophy* he intertwines labor with inheritance. To set the stage for the imbrication of labor and inheritance, Hegel emphasizes the thoroughly historical dimension of our "deeds of thinking": "As historical, these deeds of thinking at first appear to be an affair of the past, remote from *our actuality*. In fact, however, what *we* are, we are at the same time historically." And Hegel continues: "Put more precisely, just as in this domain, in the history of thinking, what is past is only one aspect, so too in what we are, our common immortality is inseparably linked with the fact that we are historical beings." Based on this decidedly historical view of what we are, it becomes necessary to invoke the pressing question of inheritance, specifically as it relates to a certain thinking of labor. "The self-conscious rationality," Hegel avers, "belonging to us and to the contemporary world did not arise directly [*ist nicht unmittelbar entstanden*] or grow simply from the soil of the present day; instead, it is essentially an inheritance [*eine Erbschaft*] and, more specifically, the result of labor [*Arbeit*], indeed the labor of all the prior generations of the human race." Whereas the *Phenomenology* seeks to describe the process of labor by means of which spirit (*Geist*) forms itself—a process that Hegel there summarizes as the labor of the concept—the emphasis here is on the ability to develop a certain receptivity in relation to the

42

work of inheritance. "This inheriting," he suggests, "involves receiving and possessing the inheritance [*zugleich Empfangen und Antreten der Erbschaft*], and at the same time reducing this heritage to a raw material that becomes transformed by spirit. In this way what is received [*das Erhaltene*] is changed and enriched, and at the same maintained [*erhalten*]." Receiving an inheritance through labor does not exclusively involve the material labor and the transmission of property and goods in the sense in which Marx and Engels would later develop their critique of political economy, an economy which they believe is to be disrupted. Rather, Hegel's attempt to mediate inheritance and labor (*Arbeit*) dialectically—also and especially, one may add, in light of the etymological and conceptual intertwinement of inheritance (*Erbe*) and labor (*Arbeit*)—is motivated by the notion that any true inheritance first must be appropriated through labor. It is only through this conceptual and concrete labor that the inheritance first becomes what it actually is, even as it is also fundamentally changed or othered (*verändert* is Hegel's word) in the process and thus becomes something else as well. It is only through the otherness into which it is changed that the inheritance comes into its own—that is, it becomes itself precisely in the moment when it is no longer simply and exclusively itself. It is, after all, only the interpretative labor of making something one's own that is capable of changing, enriching, and maintaining an inheritance *as* inheritance, a form of labor that in this manner becomes the foremost scene of an intellectual legacy.

32

Unreadabilities of Inheritance. — The specific interpretive challenge to which an inheritance exposes the heir is framed by a
double gesture that demands interpretation (thereby rendering,
through the idea of future legibility, the concept of an act of
inheriting that is based on understanding thinkable in the first
place) and simultaneously resists any attempt at interpretation
(because if the legacy to be handed down simply could be read
and understood immediately, it would not be an inheritance
in the strict sense at all, since there would be nothing to learn,
nothing to acquire, nothing to understand, and nothing to appropriate through arduous labor). In *Specters of Marx*, Derrida
helps us to understand this perspective on inheritance by stressing
the disclosive force of a legacy's retreat from legibility. He writes:
"If the readability of a legacy were given, natural, transparent,
univocal, if it did not call for and at the same time defy interpretation, we would never have anything to inherit from it ('Si la
lisibilité d'un legs était donnée, naturelle, transparente, univoque,
si elle n'appelait et ne défiait en même temps l'interprétation, on
n'aurait jamais à en hériter'). We would be affected by it as by
a cause — natural or genetic." And he continues: "One always
inherits from a secret — which says 'read me, will you ever be
able to do so?' The critical choice called for by any reaffirmation is also, like memory itself, the condition of finitude. The
infinite does not inherit, it does not inherit (from) itself." If no
inheritance is identical to itself, if it reaches the heir only ever
in the form of a dispersal of meaning which pulls consciousness
in opposite directions, and if we encounter it always under the
sign of a choice that is yet to be made, that is, a choice which

both makes the inheritance what it is and delays it as a form of futurity, then one inherits from what remains secret, the secret of reading and interpretation, which leads the heir along un-anticipatable paths. It is not clear in advance exactly where these paths might lead or, indeed, whether they lead anywhere at all.

33

Wrinkles. —Like the wrinkle in the face of my lover—which does not trigger horror within me but rather intensifies my love for her or him even more because the wrinkle shows my lover to me as temporally conditioned, which is to say as radically fragile, transitory, mortally finite and therefore all the more precious and worthy of my love—so it is precisely the finitude of the inheritance that compels me to care for it earnestly, to learn to read it *responsibly* in the light of its finitude and mine, and even to see in it a privileged figure of finitude itself.

34

Singularities of Misinheriting. — To be sure, the aporetic structure of responsibility that an inheritance places upon us extends to all instances of inheriting and as such can be understood as a general pattern. Yet the individual forms that it takes are to be gleaned from each new situation of inheriting, its special requirements for interpretation, that is, *in the idiom of the unique and the singular.* We inherit *in* language; an inheritance passes itself down *as* language; and that which is to be inherited always figures as a language in need of understanding, even and especially when it interrupts itself, suspends itself, or simply falls mute. But the language thus examined and interpreted always runs the risk of giving rise to a wrongly transmitted inheritance, a misinherited inheritance, that is, inheriting in a faulty sense or as a failure to inherit the right inheritance.

This perpetual threat of inheriting in a faulty manner or of failing to inherit the right inheritance at all preoccupies Nietzsche's Zarathustra, who represents a special kind of genealogical thinking. It is hardly an accident that the section "On the Bestowing Virtue" ("Von der schenkenden Tugend") in *Thus Spoke Zarathustra* self-consciously intertwines the thinking of genealogy with the refractory act of a reading-inheriting. There, Nietzsche writes: "Alas, much ignorance and error have become embodied in us! Not only the reason of millennia—their madness too breaks out in us [*auch ihr Wahnsinn bricht an uns aus*]. It is dangerous to be an heir [*Gefährlich ist es, Erbe zu sein*]." What is at stake in Nietzsche's reflections is not merely the critique of an overly narrow concept of reason that demands to be targeted for philosophical and experiential

47

correction. Rather, Nietzsche is careful to awake in Zarathustra the realization that the inheritance of an intellectual legacy is always already touched by the ever-present danger of inheriting a certain "madness" (*Wahnsinn*) along with it, sometimes even *instead* of it. This danger can hardly be circumvented by the intellectual tools supplied by the inheritance itself. On the contrary, the tools with which we inherit may themselves even *be* the danger. For Nietzsche, the irreducible danger of being an heir is condensed in Zarathustra's consideration of finitude and death in connection with the inheritance: "Whoever has a goal and an heir [*Wer ein Ziel hat und einen Erben*] wants death at the right time for his goal and heir. And out of reverence for his goal and heir he will no longer hang withered wreaths in the sanctuary of life." Yet, one might ask, what precisely would be "the right time" in relation to this or that goal and with respect to an heir who has been recognized as such? When would be the hour of the heir? And what kind of a goal (*Ziel*) connects the one who departs (and subsequently bequeathes) to the figure of his or her heir? If it is "dangerous" (*gefährlich*) to be an heir, as Nietzsche emphasizes, the one who is to receive what is bequeathed to him or her finds him- or herself unwittingly confronting a legacy that perpetually compels him or her to revisit these questions, which are forever intertwined with the concept and the experience of the intellectual inheritance itself.

35

Suspended Differentiations. — Even the very possibility of distinguishing between successful and unsuccessful inheriting in the act of interpretation cannot be assumed as a given. Within the act of inheriting, the possibility and the impossibility of understanding confront one another so decisively that their sharp differentiation appears to be suspended in the act of a cautious interpretive wishing-to-understand. The structure of such an inheritance becomes visible when the prison chaplain in Kafka's novel fragment *The Trial* reports to the protagonist, Josef K.: "The correct understanding of a matter and the misunderstanding of the same matter do not mutually exclude each other fully" ("Richtiges Auffassen einer Sache und Mißverstehen der gleichen Sache schließen einander nicht vollkommen aus"). Like Josef K., the heir finds him- or herself facing a problem of reading and interpretation. Invited and compelled to read and interpret always one more time, the heir also finds himself or herself inhabiting a language that also withdraws from the possibility of understanding. The experience of this perpetual withdrawal—even and especially when it appears as an injunction to excavate and secure meaning—defines the actual act of inheriting.

36

The Past Is Not Past.—From the perspective of inheritance, what we call the past emerges as the very figure of non-self-identity, a spectral legacy that steadfastly refuses to be merely what it is and what it is conventionally thought to be. It is no accident that, for William Faulkner, the "past is never dead. It is not even past," since the past lingers on in the form of a repressed or unacknowledged inheritance. If this past continues to be called a past, it behooves us to attend to its ghostly reverberations in what we consider, perhaps somewhat prematurely, the present and the future. Present and future then become visible not as temporalities fully distinct from the past, but, more precisely, as different inflections of the past's non-self-identity, that is, as variant names for the past's refusal to be or remain itself.

37

Reinvention I. — To inherit is to reinvent.

38

Reinvention II. — To reinvent is to inherit.

39

Paleonomies. — To inherit in the emphatic and disruptive sense is to engage with a paleonomy. Inheriting is both a paleonomic act and it is to speak in the language of paleonomies. In response to the question as to whether his texts should be considered as belonging to philosophy or to literature, Derrida states that his "texts belong neither to the 'philosophical' register nor to the 'literary' register. Thereby they communicate, or so I hope at least, with other texts that, having operated a certain rupture, can be called 'philosophical' or 'literary' only according to a kind of paleonomy." This "strategic necessity" fastens upon the figure of paleonomy, "the maintenance of an old name in order to launch a new concept." By extension, one might say that a paleonomy names a kind of inheritance. What is inherited is the old and long-established name of something, a designation that always already precedes the inheritor and the scene of inheriting itself; and to maintain this filiation with what precedes him or her, the inheritor keeps the name of what came before alive, signing on to a tradition of naming, as it were, respecting and affirming the historically grown dimension of what is to be inherited. But what the paleonomy also performs is a simultaneous break with the inherited tradition, in the sense that the old name or label is no longer used to signify an existing concept, but, rather, a new, reshaped, reinvented one. This paleonomic procedure is shared by all those writers, artists, and thinkers who, as creative inheritors, teach us to learn to read an old concept in a radically reconfigured way, to hear it differently from now on. In fact, the very thinking of inheritance that is operative in the present theses on inheritance can be said to be of a paleonomic type:

53

the maintenance of an old name—"inheritance"—designed to make vivid a transformed concept.

40

Imposition. — An inheritance does not inhere. It imposes itself.

41

Being Born Posthumously.—The stability, coherence, and even existence of a bequeather cannot be assumed to precede the act of transmitting an inheritance. Sometimes, the one who bequeathes has not quite been "born" yet, which is to say not yet constructed by the reading and interpreting heirs who grant him or her a certain actuality after his or her actual life has come to an end. One may say this is the case for certain authors who, after death, became widely read, even canonical, to an extent that would have been unimaginable during their lifetimes. Kafka and Benjamin come to mind in the modern context—with Kafka now being the second most worked-on literary author after Shakespeare in global scholarship—but there is a whole universe of relatively neglected writers whose fame was created by reader-heirs long after their empirical deaths. Nietzsche, too, as the thinker of untimeliness, counted himself among such belated figures. It is no coincidence that, in *The Anti-Christ*, he alludes to his own future invention by others in terms of a birth to which these reading heirs will give rise, a birth that is yet to come and that he, at the time of composing his sentences, has not experienced just yet: "Some are born posthumously." One way of glossing this statement is to say that being born posthumously means, among other things, to be *inherited* and *interpreted* by others after one's death. To be born in the hands of one's heirs means coming into existence only belatedly, after one has left one's life behind.

42

Grave Cares. — Whatever we feel when confronted with a particular legacy, it is also always tinged by cautious trepidation, even the experience of carrying a burden. What is passed on to us, far from merely adding to our fortune or providing a surplus acquisition, also imposes heavy demands on us. As we read in Charlotte Brontë's *Jane Eyre*: "One does not jump, and spring, and shout hurrah! at hearing that one has got a fortune; one begins to consider responsibilities, and to ponder business; on a base of steady satisfaction rise certain grave cares — and we contain ourselves, and brood over our bliss with a solemn brow." This solemn brow always also accompanies any joy, any sense of fortune, any affirmation that attends the receipt of an inheritance. The most extreme form of this solemn brow emerges in Brontë's reference to "certain grave cares," which not only signifies cares that are of a grave nature but also, literally, cares pertaining to a grave, such as those cares of a graveyard keeper or the deceased's heirs.

43

Un héritier. — To inherit is always also to quote; and to quote is always also to inherit. But the range of meanings this quotation acquires in its new context, the time and space of the heir, cannot be predicted or arrested in advance — or even after the fact. What does it mean to cite, as an heir, the language of a dead and historically distant bequeather — under a different cultural sign and in a transformed historical and political situation? In 2011, Jean-Marie Straub created a memorable, yet enigmatic short film, 22 minutes long, entitled *Un héritier* ("An Heir"). In it, one first sees an old man and a young man talking to each other in animated voices while walking through a forest in the Alsace region between France and Germany. In the second scene, they continue their conversation at a local restaurant, seated side by side at an outside table, while the third and final scene depicts the young man standing in front of a brick wall — apparently a kind of ruin — in the forest reading aloud quotations from a fin-de-siècle novel by right-wing French nationalist author Maurice Barrès. That novel deals with the topic of the German occupation and annexation of the Alsace region, which became, in 1871, the Alscace-Lorraine territory under orders of the German Empire. The viewer retroactively realizes that the entire conversation the two men have been having throughout the film is based on Barrès's novel, not just the third scene, where the text is explicitly cited. In the course of the first scene, when asked by the older man why he has decided to remain in Alsace, where there is so much hardship to be endured due to German oppression, the younger man answers, apparently quoting from Barrès: "I am an heir

[*Je suis un héritier*]; I have neither the wish nor the right to abandon wealth already created." Precisely wherein this wealth consists—whether, for example, it is material, intellectual, affective, patriotic, or a combination thereof—he does not say. One may argue that the reflection on the possible meanings of this "wealth" is precisely one of the tasks of the heir. At stake is not only the way in which the characters in the film inherit a dark chapter of Franco-German relations; also at stake is the filmmaker's own inheritance of Barrès's novel. The film stages the attempt by Straub, considered a far-left artist, to cite and inherit the language of a far-right author associated with a long-gone era in such a way as to find in it something other than its original nationalist fervor. By making Barrès's gestures "citable," as Brecht would say, Straub's inheritance probes their politically subversive potential as well. When Barrès's words and modes of thinking appear as citable gestures in the constellation of Straub's filmic images, they are no longer simply and exclusively what they were intended to be. Straub's strategic inheritance of a language and a comportment that are politically and epistemologically alien to him showcases the ways in which a legacy may—intentionally or unintentionally—cite the language of the bequeather to a rather different and unexpected effect. Straub, together with his late partner Danièle Huillet, would often thematize the filmic inheritance of a literary text (as in their 1987 film that takes Hölderlin's *The Death of Empedocles* as its subject) or of a musical topic (as in the 1975 film on Arnold Schönberg's unfinished opera *Moses and Aaron*) in radically experimental ways and with an eye to convention-defying formal innovation. It is perhaps this experimental way of inheriting a literary work or a musical score that lodges the question of the heir and his or her acts of citation at the core of his or her reflective engagement with a creative and intellectual legacy, even when the heir is at odds with it.

44

Inheriting Myths. — To find oneself in the position of an heir to a legacy means confronting a set of myths that have developed around that very legacy. In fact, these myths may even be the content of the inheritance itself. In such cases, a creative and rigorous act of inheriting would have to engage not only with the specific content of a particular legacy, but also with the ways in which that content is imbricated in the mythical dimension of this or that master narrative. The variegated aesthetic production of German artist Anselm Kiefer—his canvases, objects, and installations, together with his conceptual "Book Projects," photographic meditations, and mixed-media assemblages—returns again and again to the difficulty of inheriting a legacy along with its myths. His work of aesthetic inheritance poses a series of questions regarding the interconnectedness of the historical, the mythical, and the very idea of a legacy. Inheriting an uneasy German legacy and its myths, Kiefer's work asks: What is history in relation to its inheritance? What will its relation to artistic presentation have been? What are the links between strategies of aesthetic figuration, inheritance, and the politics of memory and counter-memory? What makes it possible, today, to continue to evoke the inheritance of history in a time of stasis, a moment that seems out of joint? Do the presentation and inheritance of history necessarily imply a search for lost former presences, fugitive moments of temporality that were once simply themselves and transparently comprehensible? Or may historical presentation involve the recognition that, when viewed from the standpoint of the receiving heir, these temporal moments were never simply "present" as an essence in the first place? What does it mean that the historical presents itself not as a former presence but rather in the space of intersecting traces that inscribe its genealogical shifts and movements, and that, by extension, the historical was always already—even at the time of its retroactively projected former presence, the fiction of its anteriority—a network of traces and relays to be inherited only after the fact? Must the presentation of such networks of traces assume a particular form *by necessity* or is its formal structure always already a matter of dynamic textual and ideological negotiations that remain to be thought and creatively inherited? What, then, is the form that our responsibility to historical thinking assumes when we, as heirs, can no longer in good faith take its closure and unencumbered readability for granted?

Kiefer's art engages the inheritance of history and myth by recasting conventional historicist notions of chronology, progression, and transparency even, and especially, when it explicitly confronts such ambivalent ruptures of German history as Hermann's Battle of the Teutoburg Forest or the contested legacies of German Idealism, the architecture designed by Speer for Hitler, the myth machines of Wagner and the Nibelungs or, indeed, the fate of the Jewish people in a system of state-sponsored industrial killing under Nazism. Kiefer's work is concerned with the Sisyphean task of *working through* the inheritance of history and its imbrications in the mythical: to attempt to come to terms with their ghostliness, but also to employ them as the vexed prime material out of which reflection may flow into artistic form.

One could say, therefore, that Kiefer's confrontation with the inheritance of myth—in its tendency to expose the hidden maneuvers without which mythical dissimulations are unthinkable—works to counterbalance the movement of historical myth itself. This concern places his artistic meditations on the inheritance of myth into relation with Roland Barthes's semiological reflections on the ways in which "myth has the task of giving an historical intention a natural justification, and making contingency appear eternal." But it would be a mistake to read Kiefer's art simply as a belated myth machine or as a painterly form of transparent *Ideologiekritik*. The ambivalence that traverses his work of inheritance at any moment would foreclose such typologies, connecting Kiefer to the monumental mythological image productions of filmmaker Hans-Jürgen Syberberg.

Germane to Kiefer's art of inheritance are the mute gestures that invite us to consider how the task of thinking historically is tied to a specific ethical and theoretical commitment that responds to the predicaments of his images' elusiveness. This commitment would ask viewers to assume a critical responsibility for the inability of presentation to arrest an inherited history that will not linger as a fully readable image in a moment of crisis. Kiefer's canvases, along with his forays into Object Art, link such issues to the ways in which they become affected, in the moment of presentation, by the competing demands of diverse materialities: oil, acrylics, and shellac are put into grammatical relation with sand, earth, cardboard, photographic paper, lead, straw, and other materials. This technique of imbricating a variety of materials and thematic images belongs, as a historicizing practice, to an aesthetics of subterranean relays linking objects and thoughts which on the surface seem to have little to do with one another. Indeed, there is an elective affinity between Kiefer and certain impulses of DaDaism and Surrealism. "When one connects two distant things with each other," Kiefer suggests, "there appears a line that is all the more beautiful the less this conjunction is sensible or full of meaning [*sinnvoll*];

only then does the line appear purely as a line." The haunting image of an historical legacy that emerges from the fragmented materiality of such uneasy relations is always in retreat, even as it ceaselessly calls upon us to revisit questions concerning the space in which inheritance, memory, politics, and figuration intersect.

While Kiefer's paintings are often extended meditations on legacy, history, and visual presentation in general, they remain inscribed in the conflicted discourses of a specifically German inheritance. Indeed, Kiefer's work would be unthinkable outside of the legacy that it perpetuates and ruptures all at once, and that includes proper names such as Kant, Hölderlin, and Heidegger, Nietzsche, Rilke, and Celan. His massive 1980 woodcut *Ways of Worldly Wisdom: Hermann's Battle*, for instance, places into a constellation a multitude of significant German thinkers and writers, grouping their faces around the image of a dark, strangely disfigured forest and a camp fire burning in front of it. Here, the forest imagery resonates with the pine tree (in German: *Kiefer*) that is encoded in the artist's name. And the epic German battle evoked by the picture poses a dark threat to the faces that surround the forest; in a deadly struggle, their jaw-bones (also *Kiefer*) may well be broken. In order to protect themselves, these faces might need either a god (*Anselm*) or at least a strong helmet (*Anselm*). While Kiefer's images often work to create an artistic space that is informed by the heritage of Renaissance and Post-Romantic art as well as the visual syntax of German Expressionism, these images transgress their own legacy by confronting the disasters of more recent German history, especially German fascism and the Holocaust. Here, Kiefer's interest in charred surfaces and the movement of the flame aligns him with the writings of Paul Celan, whose Shoah poem "Death Fugue" has served as a touchstone for several of Kiefer's canvases. In keeping with Kiefer's premise "not to do something synthetic, but something rupturous [*etwas Brüchiges*]," it works to intensify the rupture of history so that a new inheritance of historicity and its myths becomes thinkable.

45

Backward and Forward.—To open up to the challenge of inheritance means to open up to a tension within the directionality of its workings. On the one hand, a legacy, to the extent that it arrives from a previous elsewhere, can be interpreted and understood—if it can be understood at all—only in relation to what lies behind, what already has come to pass. On the other hand, the movement of the life wishing to achieve such understanding must proceed in the other direction, which is to say, toward a futurity that is always yet to come. Kierkegaard is one of the thinkers for whom this tension is remarkable and worthy of recording. He notes in his journal: "Philosophy is perfectly right in saying that life must be understood backwards. But then one forgets the other clause—that it must be lived forwards." Understanding fastens upon that which has already presented itself to interpretation; only in looking back on our life—both on individual experiences within that life and on the larger trajectories of our being-in-the-world—can any possible sense be made of it. This sense changes, of course, as our interpretation of our experiences changes over time. For instance, what once may have seemed like a misfortune that befell us may turn out to have been a fortunate turn of events after all; and vice versa. In that sense, what we call "experience" in life, together with our interpretive understanding of it, lives precisely in its non-fixity. Our interpretive engagements with our life are directed backwards but they must take place, of necessity, as life moves us forward. The backwardness of understanding life is always evaginated within the pocket of a life that is moving forward. To understand the workings of an inheritance would also necessitate a relentless engagement with this tension between a backward and a forward directionality.

46

Relating to an Inheritance Without Imitating. — To receive an inheritance in an open and sensitive manner without merely imitating its bequeather or mimicking the precepts of its contents is an arduous task. In an often-overlooked passage in the *Critique of the Power of Judgment* that concerns the temporally mediated connection between two different configurations of language and thought, Kant turns his attention to this particular problem of inheriting an artistic or creative legacy. In the context of his deduction of pure aesthetic judgments toward the end of paragraph 32, he elaborates the "first peculiarity of the judgment of taste" in relation to the distinction between *Nachahmung* (copy or imitation) and *Nachfolge* (succession or following). Kant asserts that "*Nachfolge*, which refers to a process, not *Nachahmung*, is the right term for all influence which products of an exemplary author or creator [*Urheber*] can exert upon others." This means that the essence of *Nachfolge* concerns itself with "taking from the same source from which the other himself took" while "learning from one's *predecessor* [*Vorgänger*]" merely "a way of behaving or relating" ("sich dabei zu benehmen"). As opposed to imitating one's *Vor-gänger* in a process of *Nach-ahmung*, a truly transformative and challenging force can be exerted by the tradition to be inherited only through *Nach-folge*, in a manner that will not merely submit to "prescriptions" (*Vor-schriften*) but, rather, participates in the "advance [*Fortgang*] of culture" through a highly mediated relationship to the so-called original or predecessor. To the extent that the one who creates in the wake of his or her predecessor, whom one might call the bequeather or testator, is involved in learning how to translate (that is, learning to be faithful to an original—and only thus really learning from it) and simultaneously to betray it by departing from it (that is, accepting as an inheritance only certain *modes of behaving*, certain ways of *relating* to something, rather than appropriating the content or vainly reduplicating the singularities of an other's work), Kant's *Nachfolge* is predicated upon an open and constantly shifting relation to the legacy of the other as precursor, a coming to terms with an inheritance that demands fidelity, even, and especially, while also forbidding it. Kant's model gives us the transformative relations among *Nach-folge*, *Nach-ahmung*, *Vor-schrift*, and *Fort-gang* to think. For him, the relations and translational acts implied in, and demanded by, these concepts are inseparable both from an engagement with the norms and conventional expectations of the notion of relation and from an interrogation of the temporal-historical structure of aesthetic experience itself. Ultimately, there can be no rigorous thinking of inheritance that would not also attempt to work through the requirements of these relational concepts of following and succession.

47

Deniers. — There are those who will insist that inheritance is merely a juridical category, one that pertains exclusively to the handing down of material objects and goods, but not to intellectual and political matters. One might call them "inheritance deniers." They have inherited a prejudice against thinking inheritance. The thought of an intellectual inheritance makes them uncomfortable, so they prefer to inherit denial while hoping to keep the specters of unsettling legacies at bay. To rephrase Paul de Man: Nothing can overcome the resistance to inheritance because inheritance itself is this resistance.

48

Something Is Taking Its Course. — What is an inheritance? What do we inherit from an elsewhere that is not our own? To whom does our inheritance correspond and respond? From whom or what do we take our ghostly dictations? If, in the grey and mysterious world of Beckett's *Endgame*, "Something is taking its course," perhaps all we can say, by analogy, is that *inheritance is taking its course*.

49

Coming After. — To think after philosophy is to think philosophy differently. Jean-François Lyotard avers: "After philosophy comes philosophy. But it is altered by the after." Any responsible heir of philosophical thought after its demise and resurrection would have to come to terms with the particular transformations brought about by this inheritance. An act of inheritance always must confront its irreducible afterness, its situatedness in the aftermath of the after. The heir is the one who continues to grapple with the implications of the insight that the before comes into being merely as an effect of the after, that is, as a retroactive invention.

50

Inheriting Learning. — To inherit something from a teacher — a true teacher — is to be inhabited by the experience of learning. Not by the acquisition of knowledge that has at its core the transmission of this or that piece of factual information, but rather by learning *as* learning. Learning how to inherit always corresponds to a learning how to learn. Perhaps we understand how to learn as little as we understand inheritance in general and the process of inheriting an intellectual legacy in particular. For both learners and teachers, the acts of learning and teaching enter this realm. Heidegger suggests that "teaching is more difficult than learning because what teaching calls for is this: to let learn. Indeed, the proper teacher lets nothing else be learned than — learning. His conduct, therefore, often produces the impression that we really learn nothing from him, if by 'learning' we now automatically understand merely the procurement of useful information." From this perspective, we might say, useful information cannot really be taught in the emphatic sense of the term, nor can it be inherited in this sense. "The teacher," for Heidegger, "is ahead of his apprentices in this alone, that he has still far more to learn than they — he has to learn to let them learn. The teacher must be capable of being more teachable than the apprentices. The teacher is far less sure of his material than those who learn are of theirs. If the relation between the teacher and the learners is genuine, therefore, there is never a place in it for the authority of the know-it-all or the authoritative sway of the official. It still is an exalted matter, then, to become a teacher — which is something else entirely than becoming a famous professor." We become teachers from whom something can be learned — that is, inherited—only when we devote ourselves to cultivating a receptivity in our students for learning as such, through our perpetual learning of how to "let learn." While this cultivation at times may seem like nothing—as if nothing could be learned or inherited from us—in reality it is the learning of learning itself, the perpetual question mark of learning that is transmitted by our most influential teachers and which, in very fortunate moments, we may then pass on to our students. This passing-on does not consist of a concrete content, nor can it be contained by what our late-capitalist, neoliberal university technocracy likes to name, in a troubling yet telling phrase, "learning outcomes." The politics of the corporate university—that is, the contemporary university that is run essentially as if it were a for-profit corporation—prefers, even in the humanities, the rigidity of such pre-established "objectives," which faculty are mandated to enshrine in their syllabi to guarantee that true learning—the kind that cannot be predicted in advance according to an a priori instrumentalist model—does not take place. True learning and its accompanying modes of letting learn are threats to the hegemonic corporate logic of today's techno-capitalist university. The passing-on that nurtures learning as letting learn consists, rather, in the transmission of a certain respect for the question mark that is real learning, in other words, a stance that affirms the dignity and value of never quite knowing *how* to learn, never being satisfied with a pedagogical program that regards the act of learning merely in terms of an algorithm to be initialized and installed, as if it were a computer application. If there is anything to be inherited from our teachers and from us as teachers, if there is a meaningful future legacy that makes itself felt between teacher and student, it is the cultivation of a frame of mind that allows learning to take place. It lets learn. It lets inherit.

51

Institutions. — To inherit is to follow the — aporetic — injunction to found institutions in the broadest sense of the term. There can be no institution without acts of inheritance; and no inheritance without structural, theoretical, or literal gestures of institution-building. "Mochlos," a text Derrida first delivered in April 1980 in New York on the dual occasion celebrating the centenary of the founding of Columbia University's Graduate School and his own receipt of an honorary doctoral degree, presents a sustained reading of Kant's essay on the idea of the modern university, "The Conflict of the Faculties." At one moment in his engagement with Kant's text, Derrida pauses in order to remark that "every text, every element of a corpus reproduces or bequeathes, in a prescriptive or normative mode, one or several injunctions: come together according to this or that rule, this or that scenography, this or that topography of minds and bodies, form this or that type of institution so as to read me and write about me, organize this or that type of exchange and hierarchy to interpret me, evaluate me, preserve me, translate me, inherit from me, make me live on," even as every such "injunction gives rise to undecidability and the double bind, both opens and closes." The moment that an heir receives, from the textual structure of the inheritance with which she or he grapples, the injunction to reinscribe and to further the principles laid out in the archive of the legacy, she or he feels a certain demand. She or he is called upon to reproduce and to bequeathe her- or himself by preserving, reinserting, archiving, in short: by institutionalizing what she or he had found in the corpus of her or his inheritance. In some cases, this may be an experimental institution of learning or a version of the classical model of the Humboldtian university—in all cases, the injunction to inherit a text or a corpus in a responsible manner demands its reinscription and perpetuation in a different context. This demand or injunction, however, is exceedingly difficult to respond to because of the radically undecidable element that always also suffuses an inheritance. To found an institution such as a university—or any community of interpreters who assemble in the name and according to precepts of certain protocols of reading—is thus one of the ways of responding to the claims made by an inheritance that wishes to be handed down and live on, but whose meaning can never be fully arrested. The inheritance must therefore be reinvented with each new act of institutionalization; it must be re-evaluated and relearned each time a group of learners and readers sets out to gather—and thus to inherit—in its wake.

52

Nonexplicative Bequeathing. —There is a form of teaching that bequeaths a certain non-mastery. In *The Ignorant Schoolmaster: Five Lessons in Intellectual Emancipation*, the French philosopher Jacques Rancière meditates on the case of the eighteenth- and early nineteenth-century pedagogue Joseph Jacotot, who decides to reject the narrative framework of the teacher as master in favor of a revolutionary mode of instruction (or, more precisely, non-instruction). Jacotot disrupts the classical model in which the masterful expert initiates the ignorant ones into the sphere of knowledge through the explication of a content that the pupils supposedly could not grasp on their own. Jacotot turns himself into the "ignorant" master that he is in order to liberate his pupils from the fiction of a system of transmission in which they acquire only what the knowing teacher doles out to them. As Rancière puts it, the "revelation that came to Joseph Jacotot amounts to this: the logic of the explicative system had to be overturned. Explication is not necessary to remedy an incapacity to understand. On the contrary, that very incapacity provides the structuring fiction of the explicative conception of the world." In other words, it "is the explicator who needs the incapable and not the other way around; it is he who constitutes the incapable as such. To explain something to someone is first of all to show him he cannot understand it by himself." And he continues: "Before being the act of the pedagogue, explication is the myth of pedagogy, the parable of a world divided into knowing minds and ignorant ones, ripe minds and immature ones, the capable and the incapable, the intelligent and the stupid." To insist on this worldview, the explicator makes use of a "double inaugural gesture." That is to say, on "the one hand, he decrees the absolute beginning: it is only now that the act of learning will begin. On the other, having thrown a veil of ignorance over everything that is to be learned, he appoints himself to the task of lifting it." Is it possible that the ignorant schoolmaster, who turns his back on the conventional model of explication in order to allow his own mode of non-knowing to facilitate the learning of his pupils, transmits an enigmatic inheritance whose power lies in the fact that it first needs to be understood by the heirs? In other words, the handed-down legacy of this or that intellectual content may be anchored in the bequeather's non-mastery of it. Like the heirs themselves, in a certain sense the true teacher-bequeather may be ignorant and unknowing in relation to the inheritance. What the heirs receive, if they receive anything at all, is a constellation of possible comportments toward the enigmatic inheritance itself, a bafflement or inability fully to comprehend. To be sure, as becomes evident in *The Ignorant Schoolmaster*, the attempt to institutionalize revolutionary modes of teaching is very likely to fail owing to the internal contradictions inherent in the wish to inscribe within an institutional framework precisely that which is meant to unsettle its canonical assumptions. Yet there is still something valuable to be learned and inherited from the story of Joseph Jacotot. Just as Jacotot transmits to his pupils precisely by refusing to transmit — that is, by refusing to teach in the guise of the knowing master — the testator, understood in the emphatic sense, is the one who, along with the content of an inheritance, transmits his own inability to reduce this legacy to a stable form of knowledge and transparent readability. If any "explicative system" survives at all, it is left up to the pupils-heirs to under- take that explication on their own, without the guardianship of a knowing bequeather-master. This is where the politics of true inheriting commences.

53

Explanations Come to an End Somewhere. — The thinking of inheritance is at work most fully when the life that is sponsored, even sustained, by it ceases to yield a stable, recognizable meaning. Precisely this ceasing, this retreat of stable sense is of prime concern to reflective heirs as they examine their life. In the autobiographical reflections collected in *Little Did I Know: Excerpts from Memory*, the American philosopher Stanley Cavell observes that "Emerson had said, early in 'Self-Reliance': 'We cannot spend the day in explanation,' a remark I persistently hear echoed in Wittgenstein's abrupt declaration, in the very opening section of the *Investigations*: 'Explanations come to an end somewhere.' Modern (professional) philosophers, with notable exceptions, have on the whole not much interested themselves in describing human life when it is not, or seems not to be, making sense." This moment of not making sense, when the heritage that traverses a life yields itself neither to conventional explanations nor to ordinary expectations of making sense, marks the site where the thinking of inheritance most precisely begins. The thoughtful heir feels compelled to take up what the common philosopher may prefer to leave aside.

54

Time after Time. — There is no interpretation of an inheritance that is not itself subject to re-interpretation. Just as I cannot arrest the meaning of an experience once and for all, any interpretation of an inheritance is liable to be revised, recast, even rescinded — since what I assumed was its "meaning" will change over time, and I may look back upon a particular experience over the years and recognize in it something quite different than what I had seen in it at previous points in time. The radical temporality of inheritance is the prime instantiation of the non-fixity of the historical past and its experiencability.

55

Inheriting Binaries. — The inheritance of Western thought is structured in terms of binaries. The thinking of binaries lies at the heart of the origins of thinking itself. Among the Pre-Socratics, Heraclitus's extant fragments already point us in this direction: "ὁ θεὸς ἡμέρη εὐφρόνη, χειμὼν θέρος, πόλεμος εἰρήνη, κόρος λιμός" ("God is day and night, winter and summer, war and peace, satiety and famine") (Fragment 67). Heraclitus is already aware of the essential supplementarity with which the two poles of the binary condition are intertwined in an abiding tension: "ταὐτό τ᾽ ἔνι ζῶν καὶ τεθνηκὸς καὶ [τὸ] ἐγρηγορὸς καὶ καθεῦδον καὶ νέον καὶ γηραιόν" ("And, as one and the same thing, there is present in us living and dead and the waking and the sleeping and young and old") (Fragment 88). The movement of inheritance reveals how these binary poles neither merely oppose each other nor come together to form a single identity, but rather serve as the precondition that makes the other side thinkable in the first place. What becomes "mine" through an inheritance arrives from an elsewhere that is typically an absent or dead other; what now belongs to me, I will pass on in the future to another other. Inheritance is the structural movement through which the logic of binary opposition is exposed and complicated. As such, it is always also the inheritance of thinking itself — its history, its structure, but also the new perspective — that allows one to see how this thinking is troubled and *how it troubles itself.*

56

Refusals Redux. — As we have seen, it is always possible in principle to refuse an inheritance, to decline to receive or accept a legacy for a variety of reasons. But often what appears to be a refusal of an inheritance in actuality is its unacknowledged or silent receipt, what one might term its negative acceptance. For instance, in some quarters of the humanities today, there is a vocal embrace of what is called "surface reading" and "post-critique." Surface reading claims to have overcome or superseded the legacy of close reading that has been one of the mainstays of literary studies, one of its primary conceptual and practical tools, and, indeed, one of its reasons for being. Surface reading, by contrast, prefers to see a text in terms of pure immanence, that is, without a trace of transcendence, which would require close reading and in-depth questioning. Post-critique purports to have overcome the inheritance of critique by believing itself to remain purely within the realm of affirmation. The Ancient Greek root of "critique," *krinein*, which means to separate and to decide, especially in a moment of *krisis*, is to be erased in favor of non-separation and abiding self-identity. The proponents of surface reading and of post-critique, however, are misguided when it comes to their inheritance. In both cases, they believe they have overcome something on whose determined repression or rejection, however, the very terms that they advance are conditioned. After all, there can be no celebration of surface reading (a superficial reading that is intertwined with a preference for superficial thinking) without its disavowed other, close and attentive reading, a reading "in depth." By the same token, there can be no post-critique without a critique of critique; as such, it keeps the legacy of critique alive—as its repressed yet structurally necessary other. Seen from this perspective, surface reading and post-critique share a form of negative inheritance: they repress or disown their inheritance as an alterity to combat and to reject. But in so doing, they keep the very terms of their rejected inheritance alive. They perform a negative acceptance of their unwanted inheritance, while believing themselves proudly to have rejected and overcome these supposedly outmoded forms of reading and thinking. The acolytes of surface reading and post-critique celebrate their supposed refusal of an intellectual inheritance by naming it, in a misguided assumption, a form of freedom. Yet in the realm of our thinking and being-in-the-world, our inheritance often has an uncanny way of refusing to be refused.

57

Recognizing the Self. — To inherit in the emphatic sense of the term — with all the contradictions, overdeterminations, resistances, and aberrations that this activity implies — always also means not merely recognizing this or that heritage but also recognizing *oneself*, in principle, *as an heir* — as someone who belongs to the group of all heirs, as someone who, like others, is one who inherits. There is something of this need for self-recognition in the confession that Derrida makes during his conversation with Elisabeth Roudinesco, in the section entitled "Choosing One's Heritage" of *For What Tomorrow* . . . : "I have always recognized myself in the figure of the heir." This self-recognition as an heir, which may energize and propel while also causing consternation, "means not simply accepting this heritage but relaunching it otherwise and keeping it alive. Not choosing it (since what characterizes a heritage is first of all that one does not choose it; it is what violently elects us), but choosing to keep it alive." To recognize oneself as an heir is therefore always also an affirmation — not of the predetermined meaning of a particular inheritance, but of a mere living-on. Such living-on keeps something alive *as such*, without any premature imposition of meaning, so that the survival of a heritage can become the focus of a laborious future interpretation and engagement in the first place. Recognizing oneself as an heir is a letting live of both oneself and the other called inheritance, as well as the other others who, as future heirs, also will be called upon to recognize themselves as heirs in their own right — when it is their turn.

58

Mitwelt. — One does not always bequeath to posterity alone. An inheritance can also be directed, consciously or nor, at one's contemporary world. As the contemporary German philosopher Peter Sloterdijk notes, "we are less and less capable of maintaining the illusion that posterity [*die Nachwelt*] will be able to pass correct judgment upon us. We are losing this illusion because we know all too well what posterity [*Nachwelt*] can achieve: After all, we ourselves are posterity [*Nachwelt*] to so much of what came before [*Vorwelt*], and we recognize that our ability and willingness to do justice to what was achieved and accomplished before us is rather lousy." He continues by suggesting that if "we already are so incompetent, how much more incompetent will be those who follow us. The consequence is clear: We must seek, as best we can, posterity [*Nachwelt*] in our contemporary world [*Mitwelt*]." Perhaps, then, the legacy of an inheritance does not always travel from a *Vorwelt* to a *Nachwelt*, from a pre-world to a post-world, but rather requires actualization and engagement in the *Mitwelt*, one's "with-world" or shared world. Yet this *Mitwelt* is not simply one's *Umwelt*, or environment; rather, the contemporaneity of one's *Mitwelt* is to be located precisely where, sometimes, the act of inheritance seeks to come to pass — or, as we occasionally happen to notice only belatedly and to our surprise, is silently already coming to pass. A writer, thinker, and teacher does not necessarily, and not always, need children, students, or so-called disciples for this mode of inheritance to make itself felt in his or her own time. In the orbit of inheritance, the legacy associated with posterity can in fact inhabit our own with-world, the "with" of our world. Inheritance refuses to be contained fully by any single wor(l)d—it is always multiple, traveling, jumping, and switching among worlds and their temporalities.

59

Refusals of Fashion.—The one who refuses to go with the previously accepted systems of his or her social world and its aesthetic codes enacts a particular refusal to inherit. In his 1967 *Système de la mode* (translated as *The Fashion System*), Barthes writes: "Every new Fashion is a refusal to inherit, a subversion against the oppression of the preceding Fashion; Fashion experiences itself as a right, the natural right of the present over the past." The refusal to inherit a fashion manifests itself as a rejection that also figures as an affirmation—an affirmation of the fashion that succeeds the previous fashion and that thus works to date it, to historicize it, and to make it momentarily obsolete. Can a true heir ever be considered fashionable and *au courant*?

60

Refusals, One More Time. — The desire to learn how to inherit responsibly is always also haunted by the specter of its other: the wish not to be affected by a heritage at all and thus tacitly to be able to signal a clear break and a fresh beginning. This ill-fated wish is extended by Paul de Man to the condition of modernity as such. "Modernity," he writes in "Literary History and Literary Modernity," "exists in the form of a desire to wipe out whatever came earlier, in the hope of reaching at last a point that could be called a true present, a point of origin that marks a new departure." It is as though a consciousness that harbors the desire to erase its own historicity, a truly meaningful and "original" form of living, feeling, and thinking, could be experienced only through a denigration and rejection of that which has formed the consciousness in the first place. But no matter how much such an attitude wishes to distance itself from the trajectory of its own formation, no matter how strongly it resists its own Nietzschean genealogy, and no matter how intensely it hopes to enthrone itself as its own origin (that is, as its own mother and father): it will continue to have to reckon with the irrepressible specters of inheritance, legacy, and transmission that make consciousness what it is and, in its ongoing engagements with its enigmatic heritage, what it may become.

61

Keeping Watch. — Among the aphorisms and fragments assembled in *The Writing of the Disaster*, Maurice Blanchot includes a one-sentence entry, italicized: *"Keep watch over absent meaning."* As in the case of inheritance, absent meaning cannot be replaced by present meaning, as if, through an act of persistence willingly performed by a sovereign consciousness, what has no meaning could be filled by a meaning imported from elsewhere. Instead, our vigilance fastens upon the need to protect the absence of meaning, not to allow it to be replaced by this or that claim of a supposed meaning. Meaning, even when it threatens to lead us astray by appearing to offer a stability that it ultimately cannot guarantee, is always on the brink of intruding on the absence of meaning. Absent meaning, too, wishes to be guarded, protected, and nourished. What we must keep watch over also includes such meaning *in absentia* as it inflects the scene of receiving an enigmatic legacy. Inheritance and vigilance go hand in glove.

62

Palliatives.—Is it possible to view the act of inheritance not exclusively as an unruly intrusion, a rogue occurrence that unsettles, but also from the standpoint of a certain experience of solace? Perhaps we would do well to heed a reflection found in Cervantes's *Don Quixote*, where—precisely during the late scene in which the protagonist composes his last will and dies—we encounter the notion that there "is a strange charm in the thoughts of a good legacy, or the hopes of an estate, which wondrously removes or at least alleviates the sorrow that men would otherwise feel for the death of friends." Cervantes helps us to ask if the prospect of an inheritance does not also work to erase the grief that makes itself felt in the wake of the death of someone who is close to us, someone who bequeathes something to us. Viewed from this perspective, inheriting a legacy or an estate can be said to help us make the transition from melancholia to proper mourning, as Freud would put it, preventing us from remaining forever mired in a state of melancholia that cannot work through a loss so as to divest libidinal energies from the departed object, idea, or person. Can an inheritance serve as a more or less unspoken palliative?

63

Little Greeks. — Some forms of inheritance assume the form of parody, in which the admiration for an unattainable former standard or achievement is intertwined, through irony, with its denigration. One may think, for instance, of the inferiority that many Romans felt with respect to their own culture in comparison with the Greek culture that preceded it and whose learning and innovation, especially in their idealized forms, appeared hopelessly out of reach. The complex Roman inheritance of Greek culture and learning made itself felt not only in such activities as the large-scale transfer of Greek artifacts and structures to Italy (where they are still on display today in a more impressive and extensive manner than in Greece itself): it also became visible in the establishment of the so-called *Graeculi* or "little Greeks." *Graeculus* was the designation for an educated person typically employed as a private tutor and teacher by members of the Roman ruling classes and their children in the first century B.C. Even though the *Graeculi* and their inheritance of classical Greek erudition were ridiculed in Rome by the likes of Cicero and Juvenal, it was also the case that it was their classical learning, lodged in the Greek legacy, that made possible the education of privileged Romans. Thus, even while they no longer belonged to the fallen empire of Greece, revered by Romans as the unattainable and long-lost ideal of cultural and intellectual sophistication, the *Graeculi*, even as mere *little* Greeks, facilitated the transmission of a level of knowledge and reflection that otherwise would not have been available to Roman culture. Through the complex dynamic of inviting and refusing a legacy, of affirming yet keeping at bay through parody and disdain, the complicated pulse of an inheritance becomes audible. In considering this form of inheriting, one cannot but recall the ironic remark that Einstein, upon arriving in Princeton, is reputed to have made when he observed that scientists, scholars, and thinkers like him were tolerated as amusing *Graeculi* by the well-meaning local savages. Are aspects of this image of the *Graeculi*, along with its complex and overdetermined relationship to a legacy that it embodies, not still relevant to a political understanding of how intellectuals and scholars, inside and outside the university, are regarded by the mainstream of their culture today?

64

Inheriting Inheritance. — There can hardly be a history of inheritance that is not itself inherited. To reflect upon inheritance always also means finding oneself inscribed, as a late-coming heir, in the movement and genealogies of the thinking of inheritance itself. To think inheritance is already to inherit.

65

Anxieties of Inheritance. — To be an heir means to be unsettled and ill at ease. It means to feel anxiety. Yet this anxiety of inheritance is not to be restricted to the general phenomenon that Harold Bloom memorably termed the "anxiety of influence" with respect to canonical writers and their predecessors, although it is genetically related to it. The question of receiving scrambled transmissions from a time that, and from a strong predecessor who, have come to pass provokes the question of how to accept and read these transmissions from an elsewhere. At stake is not merely the problem of how to keep a strong influence at bay but also how to ascertain what, in relation to the work and thinking that precede the self, can be regarded as one's own. One may think, for instance, of Schleiermacher's transformative philosophy of nature, which still understood itself, in a fundamental sense, only as coming after Fichte's defining philosophy of consciousness, or those authors who wrote in Goethe's long shadow and feared being seen merely as literary epigones, such as Keller, Platen, Stifter, and Raabe. The anxiety of inheritance is always also tied to an inchoate hope: to shape in a decisive manner the contours of an answer to an abiding Nietzschean question, the heir's genealogically inflected query of "how one becomes what one is," "wie man wird, was man ist," even as Nietzsche concedes that one still does not fully know what one is in the present.

66

Living On. — To turn toward questions of inheritance, to inquire into the spectral workings of a legacy, is one of the persistently uncircumventable ways of engaging a particular form of living on and its relation to life as such. The consideration of inheritance belongs to those critical activities that, as the early Benjamin puts it in 1919, form "part of the history of how a person *lives on* [*Geschichte des Fortlebens eines Menschen*], and precisely how this living-on [*Fortleben*], with its own history [*mit seiner eigenen Geschichte*], reaches into life [*ins Leben hineinragt*]" and becomes a matter of study for "those who come after [*die Nachkommenden*]." If the legacy of a *Fortleben*, a living-on or living-forth, which is distinct from a mere survival (*Überleben*), as Benjamin will later insist in "The Task of the Translator," possesses its own history, then that history deserves to be studied in its own right. In fact, it demands to be considered as separate from, yet standing in permanent relation to, other modes of history and genealogical inquiry. It is precisely by insisting on the history that is proper to the living-on or living-forth of a *Fortleben* that the inheritance it harbors can be studied with respect to how the living-on of an inheritance inflects life itself. Indeed, such a living-on as inheritance *is* life itself.

67

There May Be No Heir. — To reflect upon inheritance is not the same as taking the heir for granted. Just as there are cases in which there is nothing to inherit — either materially or intellectually, or both — the existence, or future existence, of heirs who will assume the legacy passed down by a testator can never be taken as self-evident. As Derrida muses during the final interview he granted shortly before passing away, published as *Learning to Live Finally*, a significant and uncomfortable question imposes itself: "Who is going to inherit? Will there even be any heirs?" In the case of a writer and thinker such as Derrida, one must be willing to consider the possibility that there is no heir. "I am ready," he confesses, "to entertain the most contradictory hypotheses in this regard: I have simultaneously — I ask you to believe me on this — the *double feeling* that, on the one hand, to put it playfully and with a certain immodesty, one has not yet begun to read me" and that "later on . . . all this has a chance of appearing." Yet, on the other hand, "I have the feeling that two weeks or a month after my death *there will be nothing left.* Nothing except what has been copyrighted and deposited in libraries. I swear to you, I believe sincerely and simultaneously in these two hypotheses." Any potentiality of a future reception, an unexpected and unplannable legacy that is yet to come, is always also modulated by the specter of the absent, missing, or extinct heir. To reflect upon inheritance means to reflect upon the possibility of the heir's radical absence.

68

Chiseling. — What at certain moments in our experience we consider our "own" identity — comprising, among other things, our views, politics, practices, preferences, beliefs, histories, routines, engagements, aversions, obsessions, interests, and pathologies — turns out, upon closer inspection, to have been inherited from an elsewhere, from someone who, or something that, came before us and is therefore not our "own," at least not in any straightforward sense. It is said that Michelangelo once was asked how he had managed to create his masterpiece sculpture, *David*. Michelangelo is reported to have responded that David was in fact always already inside the large block of marble and that all the artist did was to remove some of the material surrounding David in order to allow him to become visible. Can the engagement with inheritance be thought of in analogous terms? To be sure, considering the workings of an inheritance upon a being-in-the-world is not the same as forming a Renaissance marble sculpture. And yet, it is as if one had to chisel away, in a deliberate and crafty way, at a certain amount of surrounding material to find, at the very core, a life-formation, a set of intertwined legacies that stem from an elsewhere. These legacies typically are hidden within what we sometimes call, often prematurely and somewhat misleadingly, our identity, yet they have always already been there and they fundamentally make us who and what we are. To confront these heterogeneous and unruly modes of inheritance lodged at our core always requires persistent chiseling, which, in the process, provides a fresh vista onto Nietzsche's question as to how to philosophize with a hammer — even as there is no coherent, self-identical, and sovereign self to be found.

69

Arresting Motion. — An artist can be seen as the strategic bequeather of an aesthetically mediated inheritance to strangers who may not even have been born and whom he or she will likely never know. As Faulkner puts it in his *Paris Review* conversation with Jean Stein: "The aim of every artist is to arrest motion, which is life, by artificial means and hold it fixed so that a hundred years later, when a stranger looks at it, it moves again." Viewed from this vantage point, the artist interrupts the temporality of life momentarily in the work of art so that the life thus interrupted can live on in a distant, unimaginable futurity. The arrested motion — a life aesthetically suspended for a brief moment — comes to be handed down as an inheritance to an unknown benefactor who will be called upon by the artwork to revivify what has been frozen into form by her or his historical forbearer. The differentiation between arresting and setting back into motion maps onto the differentiation between bequeathing and inheriting — and, following the act of inheriting, the effort commences once again with a further, and each time unique, arresting of motion on the part of the heir.

Elective Affinities. — What determines the significance and impact of a work of art and of an intellectual creation more generally is inseparable from the way it is mediated by its multiple transmissions and modes of inheritance at points in time that are not coextensive with the work's immediate context. In his remarks on the relatively little-known eighteenth-century political writer Carl Gustav Jochmann, intended as an introduction to Jochmann's text "The Regression of Poetry" for a 1940 issue of the *Zeitschrift für Sozialforschung*, Benjamin observes: "The place that intellectual productions hold in the historical tradition [*in der geschichtlichen Überlieferung*] is not determined always, or even principally, by their immediate reception. Rather, they are often received indirectly [*mittelbar rezipiert*], through the medium of production left behind [*hinterlassen*] by the writers with elective affinities [*Wahlverwandte*] to the ones in question — be it as forerunners, contemporaries or successors [*Vorgänger, Zeitgenossen, Nachfolger*]." A work's potential elective affinities to those others who may inherit, or fail to inherit, the work on their own terms and in their own singular ways determines its fate. An intellectual creation is intertwined with its afterlife, that is, with the multiple ways in which it will not remain itself during the processes of transmission and reception — or lack thereof — in the realm of inheritance. The true time of a work, a refractory and substantive intellectual production, is always yet to come — in the hands of its potential inheritors, who may dwell close at hand or live hundreds of years in the future. The work's essence and substance, its survival and transmission, always belong to the other. It is thus not for nothing that Jochmann specified in his last will and testament that, upon his death, his heart was to be removed from his body and sent to his friend, the business man Konrad Heinrich von Sengbusch.

71

Letting Sentences Run Risks. — One sometimes hears a certain prejudice, usually whispered on the quiet, in German- and English-speaking academic settings about a supposed philological carelessness on the part of French scholars. They tend not to record and document, so the prejudice goes, their references and sources in the painstaking and scrupulous manner that serious scholarly work demands. Jean-Luc Nancy once responded to this view by saying: "Maybe some French have a certain lack of philological seriousness. But without trying to make excuses, one should also take into account a Nietzschean heritage or rebellion against a certain philology. Therefore, the omission was sometimes done deliberately from the outset." And he continues by offering a striking image: "You sometimes have to take books out of libraries, and sentences out of books; that is a way of giving them another chance or letting them run another risk." The Nietzschean heritage that Nancy evokes is relevant to the question of inheritance as a whole. Precisely by surreptitiously removing an intellectual legacy from its securely anchored post, one liberates it in virtue of future appropriations and reinscriptions by other heirs. Tearing a book or sentence out of context—and every citation is always already a de- and re-contextualization, a strategic transfer to the elsewhere of a discourse that takes place in a different time and space—is a way of countersigning its possible survival in a future that is yet to come and yet to be inherited. Perhaps one may even say that neglecting or erasing the traces of one's philological appropriations is not merely a scholarly aberration but also a way of setting the stage for an unexpected living on, a survival that might have been impossible if the book or sentence had simply been left alone in the supposedly proper and appropriate place, where it might have gathered dust and fallen into uninheritable oblivion. By letting books and sentences run another risk, the inheritor may rescue them for the inheritance of future heirs — that is, for futurity as such.

72

The Strength That No Certainty Can Match.—The true politicality of inheriting an intellectual or political legacy is indissociable from the premise that to inherit is to inherit without quite knowing how. In order to inherit without knowing how, it is necessary to invent modes of inheriting. If the politicality of inheriting cannot be reduced to calculation, an expectation, fulfilled possibility, a contract, an already-known way of receiving a legacy, then its thinking requires a creative act of invention. In a brief reflection, written in the aftermath of France's vehement December 1995 general strikes under the title "What Is To Be Done?"—alluding to the political inheritance of Lenin's question, vectorized in a different direction—Jean-Luc Nancy suggests that the "question places us simultaneously before a doubly imperative response," in which it is "necessary to measure up to what nothing in the world can measure, no established law, no inevitable process, no prediction, no calculable horizon" and in which it is "necessary to invent and create the world itself" without "ever knowing in advance what is to be done." As Nancy reminds us: "Invention is always without model and without warranty. But indeed that implies facing up to turmoil, anxiety, even disarray. Where certainties come apart, there too gathers the strength that no certainty can match." If inheriting also is immeasurable by the political calculations of what is merely established, that is, by a world that is already prefabricated, it belongs to that which has no model and offers no guarantees. Its possible models need to be invented, each time anew, even—and especially—if they still entertain a relationship—be it affirmative, negative, or both at the same time—to the political legacy of other models that came before them. To inherit in the strong sense means to receive the anxiety that attends any such act, the uncertainty concerning what is to be done and thought in relation to the legacy that now confronts the heir. But there is a different kind of strength at work in the act of inheriting, one that is tied precisely to its uncertainty and unpredictability. To be sure, the act of inheriting a difficult intellectual legacy tends to leave its heir in a position of radical vulnerability and unsettlement. Yet the act of inheriting under the auspices of an irreducible uncertainty always also requires the setting of a stage for the possible future reception of a strength: the strength that no certainty can match.

Fatherless Inheritance.—Boston, Fenway Park, September 2019. The current incarnation of the English rock band The Who, fronted by lead vocalist Roger Daltrey and guitarist Pete Townshend, performs a concert on their "Moving On!" tour, this time together with an orchestra. On drums for The Who is not the legendary and eccentric drummer Keith Moon, who had joined the original band in 1964 and remained with them until his untimely death from a medication overdose in 1978, but rather the younger drummer Zak Starkey, for whom Moon had been godfather. Starkey's father, Beatles drummer Ringo Starr, is reported to have given his son only a single drumming lesson ever—in an effort to dissuade Starkey from inheriting his father's legacy by pursuing a career as a musician. Instead, it was godfather Keith Moon who gifted Starkey his first drum kit at the age of eight and encouraged him to develop his talent. If Starkey now performs as the drummer for The Who in place of—and as an heir to—his deceased godfather and mentor Moon, one might also say that Starkey has assumed the mantle of a fatherless inheritance. After all, Starkey's gift for drumming, which doubtless was transmitted to him as an inheritance from his father's side, could flourish only because Starkey also rejected or ignored his father's wishes in relation to that inheritance. Starkey's father thus stands both as the source of, and as an obstacle to, the inheritance that made his son who he is. If Starkey is an appropriate heir to Moon, one might also consider him, in figurative terms, a bastard son of his actual father, whose original wish had been that his own musical inheritance, his legacy as a Beatles drummer, would not be passed on to his son. Starkey's case would seem to be a fatherless inheritance, one that is not signed or countersigned by the hand of the male parent, never signed over in testamentary form by the ancestor, never fully blessed or affirmed by the paternal superego. Zak Starkey's brilliant and haunted drumming cannot but resonate as probing echoes, embodying an orphaned remainder that leaves the (musical) heir himself something of an orphan. It is perhaps no mere accident that Zak is a short form of Zacharias, which in turns derives from the Hebrew Zechariah, meaning "Yahweh remembers." When it comes to the vagaries of a paternal yet fatherless inheritance, how could one not also listen for what God remembers every time a set of sticks hit the drum skin?

74

Speaking With the Dead. — To inherit is to engage in a sustained dialogue with the dead. The heir, if he or she is willing, enters a conversation with an absent speaker, imagining how the bequeather would have responded to particular questions or concerns the heir brings to her or him so belatedly. Inhabited by (at least) two voices at once — the voice of the self and the voice of the deceased testator — the heir negotiates a back and forth that is propelled by the on-going curiosity of the one who is left behind. The Shakespeare scholar Stephen Greenblatt once memorably suggested that the wish to converse with dead others is a significant force animating the field of literary studies. "I began," he confesses, "with the desire to speak with the dead." Even though this desire is "a familiar, if unvoiced, motive in literary studies," it typically remains "buried beneath thick layers of bureaucratic decorum." Greenblatt adds: "If I never believed that the dead could hear me, and if I knew that the dead could not speak, I was nonetheless certain that I could re-create a conversation with them." Even though it "was true that I could hear only my own voice," this voice in fact "was the voice of the dead, for the dead had contrived to leave textual traces of themselves, and those traces make themselves heard in the voices of the living," so that "even the most trivial or tedious" of traces "contains some fragment of lost life." At the same time, it is "paradoxical, of course, to seek the living will of the dead in fictions, in places where there was no live bodily being to begin with." Yet, as he surmises, "those who love literature tend to find more intensity in simulations — in the formal, self-conscious miming of life — than in any of the other textual traces left behind by the dead, for simulations are undertaken in the full awareness of the absence of the life they contrive to represent." Evoking his own experience of speaking with the dead as a reader of literature, he adds that "I found the most satisfying intensity of all in Shakespeare" and wished "to know how Shakespeare managed to achieve such intensity," for "I thought that the more I understood this achievement, the more I could hear and understand the speech of the dead." Perhaps, then, there can be no study of literature, even of contemporary literary texts whose empirical authors are still alive, without this desire to communicate with, and thus to inherit from, the dead. Shakespeare could never be inherited, the beauty and rigor of his aesthetic and conceptual achievement never appreciated, if one had no desire to speak with the dead, if one had no taste for spectral dialogues and even polylogues. In fact, no writer's claim on our attention could ever lead to an act of inheritance if the reading heir were not willing and eager to speak not simply with the living, but, first and foremost, with the departed. To be sure, in performing the particular kind of inheriting-reading that literature demands—a kind of rigorous yet free philology that derives from *philologia*, or love of words, in the best sense—one must come to terms with the realization that no empirical life was ever present in the materiality of the letter to begin with, and no retroactive reconstruction can transfigure a literary text such that it can be said to be inhabited by the pulse of an actual being. And yet, one might say that without the wish to speak with the dead—however illusory or unfulfillable that desire may turn out to be—and without the willingness to suspend one's conversations with the living long enough and regularly enough to allow for meaningful and haunted communications with the dead, there could be no sustained and rigorous attempt at inheriting a literary legacy. Indeed, perhaps there could be no such thing as a true—that is, refractory and infinitely demanding—legacy at all.

75

Two Sides of the Coin. — The heir is *always alone* because it is he himself or she herself—and no one else—who must learn to read the text of his or her inheritance in an irreducibly singular way. The heir is *never alone* because, in the act of inheriting, he or she is always speaking with others, dead or alive.

76

The Past Conditional. — The heir, as the one who survives another's demise and accepts the task of receiving an inheritance, is bound to confront the question of the bequeather's possible wishes and intentions, even though these may be impossible to ascertain and, at any rate, unlikely to conform to what a rigorous act of reading-inheriting may turn out to demand of the heir. In the novel *Nothing To Be Frightened Of,* the British writer Julian Barnes has the narrator and his philosopher brother, in the course of discussions surrounding their mother's funeral, reflect on the idea that those who survive are bound by the wishes, known or imagined, of the deceased. As the narrator observes, the "past conditional . . . is a tense of which my brother is highly suspicious." When suggesting that they should take a particular course of action based on their speculations about what their mother would have wanted, the narrator finds that his brother "took logical exception to this":

> He pointed out that there are the wants of the dead, i.e. things which people now dead once wanted; and there are hypothetical wants, i.e. things which people would or might have wanted. "What Mother would have wanted" was a combination of the two: a hypothetical want of the dead, and therefore doubly questionable. "We can only do what *we* want," he explained; to indulge the maternal hypothetical was as irrational as if he were now to pay attention to his own past desires. I proposed in reply that we should try to do what she would have wanted, a) because we have to do *something*, and that something (unless we simply left her body to rot in the back garden) involves choices; and b) because we hope that when we die, others will do what we in our turn would have wanted.

From the perspective of the surviving heir, the past conditional tense and its implications for acting in either this way or that way emerge as a matter of substantive contestation. Though the unruly legacy of a challenging inheritance whose meanings may be exceedingly difficult to read can never be reduced to an intentionality that is ascribed to the former consciousness of a bequeather, knowingly or tacitly violating what the testator may have wished still causes the scrupulous heir distress. Not wishing to betray her or his responsibility to the dead, yet unsure of the extent to which the deceased's wishes can—and, epistemo-logically speaking, should—be reconstructed as the basis for an act of inheritance, the responsible heir is caught in an aporia. To inherit an intellectual legacy in an emphatic, responsible manner also is to encounter the ways in which the supposed wishes and intentions of the dead bequeather can never be the sole guiding principles when engaging with a refractory and resistant inheritance. It is no coincidence that Benjamin emphasizes in the epistemo-critical prologue to his *Trauerspiel* study that "truth is the death of intention."

Humic Inheritance. — When engaging in the kind of thinking we do in the humanities, it always behooves us to recall the essential significance of inheritance — and, by extension, the thinking of inheritance — for all thought and experience as it presents itself to us in our lifeworld. In *The Dominion of the Dead*, the Italianist and literary scholar Robert Pogue Harrison puts it well when he reminds us of our fundamental relation to the legacy of our predecessors. "Our basic human institutions," he writes, "are authored, always and from the very start, by those who came before. The awareness of death that defines human nature is inseparable from — indeed, it arises from — our awareness that we are not self-authored, that we follow in the footsteps of the dead." This "necrocratic" disposition can be articulated as follows:

> Whether we are conscious of it or not we do the will of our ancestors: our commandments come to us from their realm; their precedents are our law; we submit to their dictates, even when we rebel against them. Our diligence, hardihood, rectitude, and heroism, but also our folly, spite, rancor, and pathologies, are so many signatures of the dead on the contracts that seal our identities. We inherit their obsessions; assume their burdens; carry on their causes; promote their mentalities, ideologies, and very often their superstitions; and often we die trying to vindicate their humiliations. Why this servitude? We have no choice. Only the dead can grant us legitimacy. Left to ourselves we are all bastards. In exchange for legitimacy, which humans need and crave more than anything else, we surrender ourselves to their dominion. We may, in our modern modes, ignore or reject their ancient authority; yet if we are to gain a margin of

real freedom—if we are to become "absolutely modern," as Rimbaud put it—we must begin by first acknowledging the traditional claims that such authority has on us.

If Harrison proposes to investigate what he calls the "humic foundations of our life world," by which he means foundations "whose contents have been buried so that they can be reclaimed by the future," he does so by focusing on the practice of burying the dead as a way both to achieve closure and to claim for oneself the place—a ground "humanized" through the corpse—in which one's dead are interred. The many secular afterlives of the dead can be examined in terms of the particular categories of place and dwelling, as Harrison does, but also in the less concrete and more elusive realm of an intellectual inheritance, a legacy that holds sway over us, even when the content of a particular heritage appears remote or ruptured. There can be no thought and no experience without a visible or invisible mediation by the dead who predate us and against whose ideas, laws, practices, premises, and modes of being in the world we measure ourselves, even if only unwittingly.

Selections. — An intellectual inheritance may work to select its own most suitable reader-heirs. Instead of an heir choosing an inheritance — or choosing whether to accept or refuse an inheritance at all — the legacy itself may select the heir to whom it will hand itself down, irrespective of the inheritor's wishes. In a conversation with the late historian Hayden White on the role of the humanities today, Richard Pogue Harrison avers: "When I think about the purpose or role of the humanities, I don't see it primarily in ethical terms. One can either remain an orphan of history or one can become the heir of a linear tradition in the plural." He adds: "Greek and Roman antiquity, world cultures, the medieval Christian culture, modernity. The more one engages in the study of the past, the more one becomes an heir to it all. And why would one *not* want to become an heir?" To which White responds: "Your metaphor is a little skewed. You can only be an heir if someone puts you in their will. And it's not true that everything inherited from the past or that comes down to us from the past is intended for us all. It may be selective in the way that Jesus told us parables are." He explains: "When he's asked by disciples, 'Why do you speak in parables when we ask you a question?' he tells them another story. And they say, 'Well, why do you tell us another story?' and he says 'Well, you have to realize that in telling a story the aim is to distinguish between those who can hear and those who cannot.'" "It's a way of selecting people," White adds, "who are prepared for very difficult truths and those who are not." One may point out first of all, with respect to Harrison's observation, that to be an heir and to be an orphan of history are not mutually exclusive. As we have seen, the heir always also stands in a kind of orphaned relation to a potentially illegible inheritance, even one that may have been intended for him. By the same token, one might not always wish to become an heir because accepting an inheritance in the emphatic sense can be laborious, treacherous, and Sisyphean in nature—not to mention the heir's trepidation before an unwanted inheritance, such as that of a criminal or aberrant parent. Yet one could also observe, in relation to White's comments, the possibility of becoming an heir even without having been written into someone else's will in explicit terms, as in the case of an intellectual inheritance in which the bequeather could not have known the future heirs of his or her thinking and writing, who may live hundreds or even thousands of year after him or her—as in the cases of haunted or spectral inheritance that we have encountered. It is possible, however, to interpret White's evocations of Jesus's telling of parables to his disciples as a commentary on the method of selecting worthy heirs for an inheritance that demands to be carefully read. If an enigmatic inheritance, not unlike Jesus's parables, requires ceaseless re-interpretation to be received by a questioning heir, then perhaps certain potential readers-inheritors are more prepared to receive a particular legacy than others. Such a proposition does not necessarily imply, as Harrison suggests—in connection with White's working-class background in Depression-era Detroit—that "education" is "precisely the means by which we force ourselves into the position of an inheritance," even when, as in White's case, a "working-class background didn't necessarily predispose you or legitimate you to be the heir of the humanist tradition of the Italian Renaissance" so that "you forced your way in there and demanded your rights to citizenship in that ideal republic." The principle of selection that is at work in an inheritance may not primarily "force" access to any particular legacy from which one otherwise would have been excluded for a variety of possible reasons. Rather, the principle of selection that is operative in an intellectual and cultural inheritance may not primarily be a tool with which a sovereign consciousness advances its aims at all. Perhaps it is the other way around. What if the selective operations of an inheritance and of a discourse of inheritance were a force of reading and interpreting that merely *came to pass or failed to come to pass*? In other words, what if the selective operations were to be regarded as the unruly inscription of a mere trace rather than a forceful act of will, even a will to power? Perhaps a powerful intellectual inheritance has a way of *choosing its own* heirs—possibly beyond the stated wishes of any one bequeather—based on their ability to rise to the task of subtly reading the internal contradictions of the legacy. While some potential heirs may never attain a rigorous and multi-layered understanding of the inheritance they are tasked with interpreting, other potential heirs may be more suited to the exacting demands of receiving the burden (and opportunities) of the internally divided, non-self-identical conundrum that is an intellectual inheritance.

79

Who Inherits?—When one considers the conceptual challenges of inheriting an intellectual legacy, does it matter who does the inheriting? Is the act of inheriting tied to a specific subject position or does it primarily unfold along discursive lines that are no longer tied to modes of sovereignty, consciousness, intentionality, and strategic control? At the end of his essay "What Is an Author?" Michel Foucault concludes his reflections with a query inherited from Beckett: "And behind all these questions, we would hear hardly anything but the stirring of an indifference: What difference does it make who is speaking?" Transposing the concern of who is speaking from the sphere of the Foucauldian "author function" to the sphere of the heir (or perhaps "heir function"), one might also ask: What difference does it make who is inheriting?

80

Dwarfs on the Shoulders of Giants. — Whenever we reflect upon something in a sustained manner, engage a particular problem, or devote our attention to a new issue that has come to concern us — that is, when we start to think — we invariably have the experience of a new beginning, as though we were about to relate to a topic in a unique and innovative way. Yet, every act of thinking, even one that feels unusually distinct and singular, is a mode of engaging with an entire network of ideas and examined concepts that came before, sometimes many hundreds of years or even millennia earlier. We find ourselves, upon closer inspection, to be dwarfs standing on the shoulders of giants. The Romans conjured this image in the phrase *nanos gigantum humeris insidentes.* In various modulations, this notion has circulated through Western thought for a very long time, including, prominently, in Bernard of Chartres during the twelfth century, and, later, in Isaac Newton, who confessed in a letter: "If I have seen further, it is by standing on the shoulders of giants." This gesture can be seen as an act of inheriting in which the heir can be said to profit by expanding upon the insights and labor that have been handed down by those who came before her or him. Yet the heir cannot take her or his position as an enterprising dwarf on the shoulders of giants for granted because the possibility remains that her or his mind is too ordinary to acquire was has been bequeathed by her or his formidable predecessors. Quite possibly, the heir is more akin to the repulsive creature in part III of Nietzsche's *Zarathustra* that is described as a "crippled hybrid" riding on Zarathustra's shoulders as he ascends a mountain. The grotesque being, "half dwarf, half mole" ("halb Zwerg, halb Maulwurf") is shown as "lame" (*lahm*) and "paralyzing" (*lähmend*) and as "dripping lead through my ear and leaden-drop-thoughts into my brain." Even though he carries ("obwohl er auf mir saß") the parasitic mole-dwarf up enormous mountain heights on his shoulders, Zarathustra is horrified by the creature who fails to appreciate what is wrought on his behalf, namely, the magnificent view that is opened up. As an intellectual heir, one may say that one stands as a proud dwarf on the shoulder of giants, or, just as likely, as an ugly and uncomprehending mole-dwarf who, even though he or she rides on the shoulders of giants, is incapable of understanding and affirming what has been offered. A certain mediocrity, lack of courage, or attachment to convention may incapacitate his or her thinking. So, how can we distinguish a forward-thinking heir-dwarf from dreadful and non-comprehending mole-dwarf? Or do the two figures coincide? One cannot always tell.

81

Translation I. — There is no inheritance that is not also an act of translation, and no translation that is not also an act of inheritance.

82

Translation II.— An act of inheritance, understood in the
emphatic sense, translates inheritance precisely *as* inheritance.

Haunting Inheritance. — Extending the haunted and haunting structure of inheritance — its spectrality, as Derrida might say — makes it possible to forge connections with the more general concept of Being. One might even hear Heideggerean echoes in Derrida's evocation of the concepts of Being and inheriting when he writes: "*To be . . .* means *. . . to inherit*" ("*Être . . .* cela veut dire *. . . hériter*"). Having thus equated Being and inheriting, Derrida continues: "All the questions on the subject of being or of what is to be (or not to be) are questions of inheritance. There is no backward-looking fervor in this reminder, no traditionalist flavor. Reaction, reactionary, or reactive are but interpretations of the structure of inheritance." If Derrida establishes an equivalence between Being and inheriting, he does not do so in order to revive tropes of traditionalism such as the cult of the dead, a transfiguration of the past, or even such absurd ideas as a so-called *Ahnenerbe*, an idealized "ancestral heritage," which the German National Socialists so blindly espoused. Owing to its non-identity, inheritance resists instrumentalization either as an identity-founding principle or as a form of self-legitimization that appropriates the past to further the agenda of a narrowly defined self-interest. Conjuring inheritance as a form of mourning and Being is not the same as coopting inheritance as a self-enriching strategic appropriation that assumes the status of a mere possession — a kind of *Dasein*-property. The necessity of making this distinction is presumably also one of the reasons why Derrida adds:

> That we *are* heirs does not mean that we *have* or that we *receive* this or that, some inheritance that enriches us one day with

this or that, but that the *being* of what we are *is* first of all inheritance, whether we like it or know it or not. And that, as Hölderlin said so well, we can only *bear witness* to it. To bear witness would be to bear witness to what we *are* insofar as we *inherit*, and that—here is the circle, here is the chance, or the finitude—we inherit the very thing that allows us to bear witness to it. As for Hölderlin, he calls this language, "the most dangerous of goods," given to man "so that he bears witness to having inherited / what he is [*damit er zeuge, was er sei / geerbt zu haben*]."

If Being-in-the-world means Being-an-heir, no right to an existing or expected property can be derived from this—no principle of identity, no cult of having been chosen, no privileged position. Rather, the concept of inheritance merely names the circumstance in which one unwittingly finds oneself. This thinking (a kind of *Nach-denken*) about finding oneself (a *Vor-finden*) therefore is, rather, an act of testimony or bearing witness to what, within us, inscribes itself as the condition of having-inherited that determines our Being-in-the-world. This, we might say, is precisely the point of Hölderlin's fragmentary draft from 1800, which Heidegger also cites in his elucidations of Hölderlin. What *Nach-denken* finds before itself (*vor-findet*) is language. And it is language itself that both enables and renders impossible a thinking that makes our Being-in-the-world visible and experienceable as a multitude of competing and hetero-geneous legacies.

Yet this double movement of mourning and bearing witness, which is proper to each inheritance and every heir, cannot elude its haunted legacy. "One never inherits," Derrida suggests, "without coming to terms with [*s'expliquer avec*] some specter, and therefore with more than one specter. With the fault but also the injunction of more than one." The specter, which in

Derrida's reading not only refers to Shakespeare's Hamlet but also can be extended to encompass the logic of a haunting inheritance more broadly, signifies an ambivalence and polyvalence within a legacy, an excess of meanings that harbors the possibility of grasping new, previously unknown levels of meaning but also the possibility that any interpretation might find itself shipwrecked on the shores of deferred meanings. Such danger is, in Derrida's logic, not merely an obstacle to be overcome but, rather, the very condition of possibility for any act of inheriting in the emphatic sense. This is why he argues: "Guaranteed translatability, given homogeneity, systematic coherence in their absolute forms, this is surely . . . what renders the injunction, the inheritance, and the future—in a word the other—*impossible*. *There must be* disjunction, interruption, the heterogeneous if at least there must be, if there must be a chance given to any 'there must be' whatsoever, be it beyond duty." Like Kant before him, Derrida brings inheriting into syntactical relation with translating. One could, in the case of inheritance, speak of a carrying-across (an *Über-setzen*) from one shore to the other, from one domain of applicability to the other. It is precisely the untranslatability, the *Un-übersetzbarkeit* of the inheritance, its interruptions and derailments, that make it appear as absolutely other.

But what can the terms "must" or "there must be" mean in this context, a "must" even beyond duty, that is to say, beyond any relation to a normative moral law? If inheritance is to be thought in terms of a responsibility in relation to a "must," would such a thinking not require a concept of inheritance that is translatable, readable, and accessible—so as to be capable of bringing moral thinking and action clearly to the fore? On the contrary, Derrida would claim that the mere appropriation of something that is transparently accessible does not cast the question of a radical responsibility into sharp relief. Rather, the concept of responsibility that is at stake here proceeds from an aporetic situation in which it is difficult, even impossible, to come to a decision that occasions a true, which is to say, metaphysically and normatively grounded, responsibility. "There is no inheritance without a call to responsibility" ("Pas d'héritage sans appel à la responsabilité"), Derrida reminds us, for an "inheritance is always the reaffirmation of a debt, but a critical, selective, and filtering reaffirmation, which is why we distinguished several spirits." If it is always the ghosts and specters that recall us to our debt, if it is always a matter of differentiating among several specters, and if any reaffirmation is oriented not toward confirming what is completed and given but rather toward an active evaluating and selecting, then the call of the responsibility thus conceived becomes audible response-ability, which is always looking for a response even as it responds to, becomes a matter of answerability to, a call from elsewhere. When viewed from this perspective, a responsibly interpretative form of inheriting becomes recognizable not only in its epistemological dimensions but also in its ethico-political embeddedness. There can hardly be an heir in the emphatic sense who could or would refuse the demands of ethics and the political—on the contrary. Yet in the sense developed here, the heir's thought and action are no longer guided by normative or prescriptive concepts of ethics and politics. The heir must invent—that is, inherit—them anew.

84

To Read What Was Never Written. — There are forms of inheritance that demand to be understood without the benefit of a last will or testament. In navigating such a refractory legacy, the heir is enjoined to act *as if* there were a testament to be read and deciphered, that is, *as if* it were possible, in principle, to make sense of the inheritance though patient interpretive engagement. Such a constellation may be one of the most forceful instantiations of Benjamin's insistence, encoded in a citation from Hugo von Hofmannsthal, that we learn "to read what was never written" ("Was nie geschrieben wurde, lesen").

Inheriting a Future. — To inherit is to inherit a future. Even though what in a traditional register would be called the "content" of an inheritance might be understood as stemming, in one way or another, from the past, the labor of engaging with a legacy always also makes it a matter of futurity — of the heir's own future and even of the future of generations to come. The contemporary Scottish artist Katie Paterson has created a remarkable work of art, *Framtidsbiblioteket* (*Future Library*), which unfolds on the timeline of 100 years (2014–2114). Situated in Nordmarka, a forest on the outskirts of Oslo, this eco-artwork consists of 1,000 newly planted trees, which, as Paterson's website explains, "will supply paper for a special anthology of books to be printed in one hundred years' time. Between now and then, one writer every year will contribute a text, with the writings held in trust, unpublished, until the year 2114." At this Norwegian location, "tending the forest and ensuring its preservation for the one hundred year duration of the artwork finds a conceptual counterpoint in the invitation to each writer: to conceive and produce a work in the hopes of finding a receptive reader in an unknown future." The first author to contribute to the project, during the year of its inception in 2014, was Margaret Atwood. As Paterson reflects, "*Future Library* is a living, breathing, organic artwork" that will "live and breathe through the material growth of trees," almost as if "the tree rings" were "chapters in a book." "The unwritten words, year by year" call to be "activated, materialized"; and the "visitor's experience of being in the forest, changing over decades" is modulated by an awareness of "the slow growth of the trees containing the writers' ideas like an unseen energy." According to the artist's plan, the writers' manuscripts "will be held in trust in a specially designed room in the New Deichmanske Library, opening in 2020 in Bjorvika, Oslo. Intended to be a space of contemplation, this room will be lined with wood from the forest. The authors' names and titles of their works will be on display, but none of the manuscripts will be available for reading—until their publication in one century's time." One might say that *Future Library* points to modes of inheriting that are yet to be invented, activating legacies—from book printing to sustainable ecology, from the genealogy of literature to addressing a future of unknown and radically uncertain heirs—whose timeframe is just beyond our immediate reach. As the artist avers, "*Future Library* has nature, the environment at its core—and involves ecology, the interconnectedness of things, those living now and still to come. It questions the present tendency to think in short bursts of time, making decisions only for us living now." To which she adds that the "timescale is one hundred years, not vast in cosmic terms. However, in many ways the human timescale of one hundred years is more confronting. It is beyond many of our current lifespans, but close enough to come face to face with it, to comprehend and relativize." It is through such artistic engagements with the questions of legacy—which will also change and transform in as yet unpredictable and un-programmable ways as the life of the artwork unfolds—that both the working-through and working-with of a past and the radically future-oriented aspect of an inheritance are cast into sharp relief. These questions of inheritance—if they are indeed to be questions of futurity—require our constant vigilance, patience, tending, care, and questioning interpretation.

86

Archival Traces. — No inheritance without archive. The archive, as that which both delimits forthcoming acts of inheritance and first opens them to a possible futurity, names the intersection of traces that inscribe, record, and store — or refuse to inscribe, record, and store — what can and what cannot become a potential object of inheritance. In his last seminar, devoted to *The Beast and the Sovereign,* Derrida speaks of the archive in terms of a "survivance" that is "broached from the moment of the first trace that is supposed to engender the writing of a book. From the first breath, this archive as survivance is at work." This structure ultimately is operative not merely "in books," "in writing," or in "the archive in the current sense," but rather in "everything from which the tissue of living experience is woven. . . . A weave of survival, like death in life or life in death." The traces that an archive gathers like marks and inscriptions in a large file, like entries in an extensive dossier, or like sentences in a book are offered up to the precarious and unpredictable modes of survival that mark the act of inheriting. Speaking of the particular case of Defoe's *Robinson Crusoe,* Derrida reminds us that the "survival, thanks to which the book . . . has been handed down to us, has been read and will be read, interpreted, taught, saved, translated, reprinted, illustrated, filmed, kept alive by millions of inheritors — this survival is indeed that of the living dead." This is the case to the extent that, as with "indeed any trace," "a book is living dead, buried alive." After all, "each time we trace a trace, each time a trace, however singular, is left behind, and even before we trace it actively or deliberately, a gestural, verbal, written, or other trace," "this machinality virtually entrusts the trace to the sur-vival in which the opposition of the living and the dead loses and must lose all pertinence." In other words, the "book lives its beautiful death," which is to say "the chance and the threat of finitude, this alliance of the dead and the living." The archive of traces to be inherited as that which may survive undermines the strict distinction between life and death, neither quite dead (although it may have passed on or been largely forgotten) nor fully inscribed in life (as if it had not already been touched by its own finitude). What there is to be inherited—if, indeed, there is anything to be inherited at all—is a matter of the archive.

87

Invisibilities. — In 1903, the Austrian art historian Alois Riegl defined the monument or memorial (the German *Denkmal,* or "mark for thinking," "mark for commemorating") "in its oldest and most primordial sense as a work made by human hand that has been erected for the specific purpose of keeping present and vivid, in the consciousness of subsequent generations, particular human acts or destinies [*menschliche Taten oder Geschicke*], or combinations thereof." A memorial, one might say, is intended as an act of cultural, intellectual, and historical transmission — a marker and purveyor of commemorative inheritance. Yet, one might add, precisely by commemorating the extraordinary by means of the ordinary, by transmitting the singular noteworthiness of something into the experience of quotidian life, the act of inheritance also always threatens to be disrupted. It is as though what the memorial wishes to give us to think and to remember were an inheritance ironically withdrawn from us — through overexposure, normalization, and inscription into the everyday routine. It is as if we were blinded precisely to what we see every day, unable to "inherit" what is too close at hand. It is no coincidence, as Robert Musil reminds us in the course of his own act of self-inheritance, *Nachlaß zu Lebzeiten* ("Literary estate while still alive") that "nothing in the world is as invisible as memorials" ("Es gibt nichts auf der Welt, was so unsichtbar wäre wie Denkmäler"). To inherit, if such a thing is possible at all, always also entails exposing oneself to the threat of an inheritance becoming invisible and gradually retreating into oblivion. Which is to say: If there is inheritance, it comes to pass *in spite of.*

88

Refunctionalizing I. — Whether one is aware of it or not, to inherit is always also to refunctionalize. It was Brecht who coined the German term *Umfunktionierung*. It can be translated variously as refunctioning, refunctionalization, radical restructuring, or functional transformation. In Brecht's thinking and in his practice as a stage director, *Umfunktionierung* involves lifting an idea, thought, concept, or practice out of its usual, expected, or original context in order critically to mobilize it elsewhere, strategically inscribing it in a different constellation and using it in the pursuit of different aims. Freed from its original or conventional setting, the object of an *Umfunktionierung* "inherits" the past of its previous life in such a way as to shed critical light on a set of different concerns in its new life. Such an act may involve, for instance, the radical adaptation of a classical dramatic text by a writer or director who has rather divergent political or aesthetic goals in mind; yet in principle it can involve any transplantation (which also involves a restructuring transformation) of an older idea into an environment in which it is not native. In an expanded sense, *Umfunktionierung* also can refer to the inheritance of a historically specific designation or political label that is mobilized to signify under different auspices, such as the symbol of the pink triangle, which was originally sewn onto inmates' uniforms in Nazi death camps to identify homosexual men — analogous to the yellow star of David demarcating Jewish prisoners — and which has since been refunctionalized as an emblem of LGBTQ pride. Such creative, courageous, and historically attuned acts of *Umfunktion-ierung* are at work — at times explicitly, at times silently — in any emphatic and deliberate inheritance of a legacy.

89

Refunctionalizing II. —When considering the relationship between the notion of inheriting and the idea of refunctionalizing, it behooves one to stress the significance of the fact that the imagined future of what is refunctionalized cannot make do without the past. In other words, whatever future-directed gestures may be at stake both in refunctionalizing and in inheriting, these gestures are inevitably inflected by the multiple complex ways in which they are rooted in what has come to pass. As the early Marx writes in "For a Ruthless Criticism of Everything Existing" (1844), those who think with him "do not attempt dogmatically to prefigure the future, but want to find the new world only through criticism of the old." Such "*ruthless criticism of everything existing*" can be thought of as ruthless "in two senses: The criticism must not be afraid of its own conclusions, nor of conflict with the powers that be." Inheriting, in the emphatic sense of the term, also means a relentless critical engagement with the old—that is, with the concepts, ideas, and objects that stem from an old or deceased testator that are now found stranded on the shores inhabited by the orphaned inheritor. What inheriting shares with the mobilization of critique is that it must direct its critical gaze backward in order to move forward. And such looking forward by looking backward can be effective only if it is unafraid of what it will encounter in its critical engagement with the past and with the modes of thought that the past has handed down. This double mode of looking must not fear the political consequences of its critical modes of inheriting—especially if and when they draw the ire of the powers that be.

90

Forgetting One's Language, Making History. — To engage philosophically with the realm of the political, an heir must learn how to think the multiple ways in which language, history, and inheritance are inexorably intertwined in the work of interpretation without assuming a merely affirmative or mimetic, but rather a refractory or even transformative, relation to what is and to what has been. Keenly aware of the particular historical, theoretical, and political difficulties and potentialities embedded in the larger concepts of inheritance, legacy, and transmission, Marx, in *The Eighteenth Brumaire of Louis Bonaparte*, first published in New York in 1852 in the German-language journal *Die Revolution*, writes:

> Human beings make their own history, but they do not make it as they please [or "voluntarily"— "aus freien Stücken"]; they do not make it under self-selected circumstances, but under circumstances existing already, given and transmitted from the past. The tradition of all dead generations weighs like a nightmare on the brains of the living. And just as they seem to be occupied with revolutionizing themselves and things, creating something that did not exist before, precisely in such epochs of revolutionary crisis they anxiously conjure up the ghosts of the past to their service, borrowing from them names, battle slogans, and costumes in order to present this new world-historical scene in time-honored disguise and borrowed language. . . . In like manner, the beginner who has learned a new language always translates it back into his mother tongue, but he assimilates the spirit of the new language and expresses himself freely in it only when he moves in it without recalling the old and when he forgets his native tongue in it ["sobald er sich

ohne Rückerinnerung in ihr bewegt und die im angestammte Sprache in ihr vergißt"].

What kind of interpretive relation to the historicity of a political phenomenon can be said to emerge in Marx's richly textured passage? The history in which heirs finds themselves is both self-made ("Human beings make their own history"; "Menschen machen ihre eigene Geschichte") and hetero-nomous, determined by a transmitted elsewhere ("not . . . under self-selected circumstances, but under circumstances . . . trans-mitted from the past"; "nicht unter selbstgewählten, sondern unter . . . überlieferten Umständen"). In order for the invention of a new world and the forging of a history to come—that is to say, always an irreducibly *singular* history ("own history"; "eigene Geschichte")—to be possible, a certain relation to the tradition of all dead generations imposes itself, demanding to be confronted. But this confrontation is not merely one of sifting and choosing, in an effort to employ, for the purposes of world-creation and of a revolutionary transformation of what is, those elements in the tradition that strike one as useful, while discarding the other, less attractive elements. Rather, taking on the tradition to be inherited, along with the "circumstances transmitted from the past" ("*überlieferten* Umstände") of the world that is, propels the heir to engage in an infinite spectral struggle, in which the "ghosts of the past" ("Geister der Ver-gangenheit") insert themselves in altogether uncontrollable ways. When the revolutionarily-minded heirs thus believe themselves to innovate, they may in fact merely be repeating; when they wish to depart from a historical scene in order to inaugurate another, new "world-historical scene," ("Weltgeschichtsszene"), they may in fact be employing, albeit unwittingly, the very same instruments and props that belong to the world which has been deemed in need of transformation in the first place. If there is a politics of freedom to be found in the singular world-making of the historical subject-as-heir, this freedom is predicated upon a rigorous and interminable interpretation of an heir's relation to the tradition and transmission that always comes from an else-where, an other. The stakes of this negotiation of freedom are high because, on the one hand, the negotiation of a powerfully transformative relation to an inherited world is the condition of possibility for any new, self-made world to come; and, on the other hand, a neglected, underdeveloped, even repressed relationship to that inheritance causes an enormous weight—a weight, in fact, of nightmarish proportions ("lastet wie ein Alp" is Marx's German phrase)—to oppress the heir and to threaten to derail any revolutionary transformation of what is. Marx employs the rhetorical image of learning a second language and the eventual freedom of no longer having to retranslate into the language into which one was born—which is to say, into the historical and material circumstances that one has inherited—in order to advance the notion of a politics of inheritance that is characterized by a dynamic and vicissitudinous interplay between knowing and forgetting. The process of forgetting what is my own, the process of liberating myself from what is an effect of a "native language" ("angestammte Sprache"), the process of recoiling from the need for any perpetual "recalling" ("Rückerinnerung") of what I believed to be my own, is thus one of the names for the inchoate, yet indomitable intimation of a certain freedom to remake, which is to say, to create a world. It is in forgetting my language—forgetting my language in the other—that I, as an heir, make history.

91

Inheriting a Contested Provenance. — The 1937 destruction of the Basque Country town of Guernica by the German Luftwaffe inspired Picasso to paint one of his best-known masterpieces, the huge and haunting canvas simply entitled *Guernica*. When, later, in Nazi-occupied Paris, Picasso was asked by a German officer who happened to see a photograph of the work at the painter's place, "Did you do this?," Picasso reportedly answered: "No, you did." Similarly, when the American comic book artist Art Spiegelman was asked, in relation to his graphic novel *Maus* — first created over the course of the 1980s — by a German journalist if he did not think it was in bad taste to have done a comic book about Auschwitz, the artist answered: "No, I thought Auschwitz was in bad taste." There are times when questions of conceptual provenance — and the attendant questions of attribution as well as the evaluation and interpretation of such attribution — strike at the heart of the inheritance of history.

92

Reading Inheriting. — Whatever else may be said about the act of reading the resistant "text" of a refractory inheritance, it can proceed only exceedingly slowly, sentence by sentence — perhaps not entirely unlike Barthes's line-by-line reading in *S/Z* of Balzac's short story "Sarrasine." True inheriting is a form of what Nietzsche names "the great, the incomparable act of reading well."

93

Understanding Tropes.—In order to relate to an inheritance, the heir needs to learn a sensitive reading of tropes. This slow and conscientious engagement with her or his inheritance opens onto the tropological nature of language itself. While it may be difficult to ascertain if the true heir can ever really belong to any particular group (unless it be the community of those who have no community), it is possible to say with certainty what group she or he does not belong to. In the chapter of *The Conduct of Life* entitled "Culture," Ralph Waldo Emerson memorably describes such a group as follows: "There are people who can never understand a trope, or any second or expanded sense given to your words, or any humor; but remain literalists, after hearing the music, poetry, and rhetoric, and wit, of seventy or eighty years. They are past the help of surgeon or clergy." Emerson continues: "But even these can understand pitchforks and the cry of fire! and I have noticed in some of this class a marked dislike of earthquakes." The true heir cannot be a literalist; he or she must remain open to the tropological earthquakes that threaten to shatter any literal and stable meaning when one least expects it.

94

Je suis, I am — Do You Follow? — Inheritance consists in the act
and experience of following, since the heir — in a temporal, experiential, phenomenological, and structural sense — is someone
who follows. One might even say that the very *being* of an heir
is inseparable from the multiple ways in which she or he comes
after something else, such as the death of the bequeather or the
transmission of an estate or inheritance. In one of his last texts
(a bequeathal of sorts), devoted to the question of the animal,
Derrida happens to point out that the French phrase "je suis"
can mean either "I am" or "I follow," depending on whether
it is understood to be the first-person singular conjunction of
the verb *être* (to be) or of the verb *suivre* (to follow). To be is to
follow. Commenting on the interconnectedness of these two
formulations, he suggests that "I am (following) this suite [*je suis
cette suite*], and everything in what I am about to say will lead
back to the question of what 'to follow' or 'to pursue' means,
as well as 'to be after,' back to the question of what I do when
'I am' or 'I follow,' when I say '*Je suis.*'" If, from this perspective,
being and following are always imbricated, making us who we
are, in terms that we never fully control or comprehend, we
might say that such issues "involve thinking about what is meant
by living, speaking, dying, being, and world as in being-in-the-
world or being-within the world, or being-with, being-before,
being-behind, being-after, being and following, being followed
or being following." One might add that, as heirs confronting
the daunting challenge of coming to terms with a potentially
unreadable inheritance, all of us say "je suis" — even when we
are not speaking French. To inherit is to follow — just as to be

is to follow, and to inherit is to be. As heirs, we come to understand ourselves as the beings who fundamentally *follow* and who are enjoined to reflect upon this enigmatic following.

95

Parusia.—Inhabiting the margins between times and their tenses, inheriting is a form of parusia. As a rhetorical term, parusia—not to be confused with the metaphysical term *parousia*, which has the same etymological root but refers to Being as presence and arrival—names the speech that employs the grammatical present tense in place of the past or future tense. The language of inheritance takes place in the present tense, the here and now of its intensity, in order to refer to experiences and events in times that have passed as well as in an imagined, yet-to-be-lived futurity.

96

Possibilities of Prosopopoeia. — On his deathbed, Brecht surprised the clergyman and publicist Karl Kleinschmidt, who was visiting him, with a remarkable and seemingly strange statement: "Write that I was recalcitrant and that I intend to remain so after my death, too. For, even then, there are certain possibilities" ("Schreiben Sie, daß ich unbequem war und es auch nach meinem Tod zu bleiben gedenke. Es gibt auch dann noch gewisse Möglichkeiten"). What could Brecht mean by this? In what, precisely, may such "possibilities" following one's own demise consist? The possibilities that Brecht believes continue to exist even after an author's empirical death unfold on the level of inheritance. The legacy of a writer will be determined in unpredictable ways by future readers and heirs, so that the recalcitrance, difficulty, and political provocation that a writer's work may have enjoined already during his or her lifetime extend beyond his or her finitude as such. If not exactly determined by an explicit testament that could ensure the execution of a bequeather's last will among those who follow, an author's refractory and resistant writing and thinking can, in fact, themselves be saturated by potentiality in ways that the departed author could not have pre-programmed but that may nevertheless create a futurity of disruptive reflection. The voice Brecht imagines on his deathbed coincides with the rhetorical figure of *prosopopoeia*, a voice from beyond the grave, uttered through the mask of an absent or dead speaker. There is, in other words, a *prosopopoeaic inheritance* that cannot be thought in separation from future possibility, even as it bespeaks — and speaks out of — death.

145

97

What's the Difference, Kafka?—Engaging with the inheritance that is handed down to us through the generations always also involves relating to our own death and to finitude itself. As Kafka notes in his so-called octavo notebooks on February 10, 1918: "The chain of generations is not the chain of your being [*Die Kette der Generationen ist nicht die Kette Deines Wesens*], and yet there are relations. Which ones? The generations die like the moments [*Augenblicke*] of your life. What's the difference?" What is handed down to us by the chain of generations is not simply the content of this or that inheritance, a particular legacy to be refuted or assumed. Rather, the chain of generations orients us to the temporality of our own being-in-the-world and to our eventual passing. Soon enough we, too, will be part of a generation that has come to pass, in other words, that has joined all the previous generations in their passing. We may recall the Latin locution for dying, *ad plures ire*, literally "to go to the many." If Kafka ends his notebook entry on the chain of generations with the question "What's the difference?", he places an interpretative conundrum before us. Is the question "Worin liegt der Unterschied?" meant to inquire into the possible ways of differentiating between the chain of generations that die and the dying moments of our lives, thereby affirming that there is in fact a difference? Or does Kafka's question, posed in a rhetorical or figurative mode, suggest that he does not really think there is a difference at all? And what, in turn, would be the difference made by our attempting to ascertain what the different meanings of "difference" might engender? These questions themselves are part of the legacy that we inherit from Kafka and that will not cease to remind us of the ways in which our own acts of inheriting are deeply imbricated with those of previous and future generations in relation to finitude.

98

Inheritance Would Be a Good Idea. — Has there ever been inheritance in the emphatic sense? Mahatma Gandhi famously is said to have responded to a journalist's question regarding his own thoughts on Western civilization by stating: "I think it would be a good idea." Perhaps something analogous can be said of inheritance: It would be a good idea.

99

Quotation. — To quote is a form of inheriting. It lets another speak openly within the discourse that is supposedly ours. The basic hospitality to the other that a quotation embodies is not lost on the reflective heir.

100

Today. — The act of inheritance bestows meaning(s) on what the heir inherits. Prior to an active, interpretative inheriting, the object of inheritance appears, if it appears at all, as a mute and distant thing. Its relevance remains obscure. When Emily Dickinson in an 1862 letter to Thomas W. Higginson insists that "Today, makes Yesterday mean," she touches upon a structure without which an emphatic inheritance can hardly be thought. Only from the standpoint of the laborious act of inheriting in which heirs are engaged — and in which they are situated always according to the terms of their own temporality, the now-time of their reading-inheriting — does the legacy of their object of reflection come into potential legibility. Only from the perspective of the act that is occurring always *today* does an intellectual heritage come to speak and to resonate beyond the confines of its occluded past. Through innovative acts of reading, translation, commentary, critique, republication, celebration, reinscription, discussion, teaching, adaptation, etc., the heir retroactively causes the otherwise silent object of an inheritance to signify.

101

Teacups. — A vigilant, rigorous, and free heir in the emphatic sense relates to the things that are handed down by an inheritance in a manner that is not merely utilitarian or guided by the narrow precepts of instrumental reason. The complex things that offer themselves up for inheritance become, in the hands of their sensitive interpreter, objects of contemplation. In the course of reflection, the multiple and irreducible meanings that suffuse the inherited thing are themselves thematized as objects of a dynamic legacy that may have continued for generations, demanding ever-renewed attention. In relating to the culture that the inherited things embody, the heir is inscribed in complex negotiations that revolve around what it means to inhabit this world with other life-forms as well as with things. As the American philosopher Hubert Dreyfus eloquently observes in the course of his engagement with Heidegger: "Our everyday know-how involves an understanding of what it is to be a person, a thing, a natural object, a plant, an animal, and so on. Our understanding of animals these days, for example, is in part embodied in our skill in buying pieces of them, taking off their plastic wrapping, and cooking them in microwave ovens. In general, we deal with things as resources to be used and then disposed of when no longer needed. A Styrofoam cup is a perfect example. When we want a hot or cold drink it does its job, and when we are through with it we throw it away. This understanding of an object is very different from what we can suppose to be the Japanese understanding of a delicate, painted teacup, which does not do as good a job of maintaining temperature and which has to be washed and protected, but which is preserved from generation to generation for its beauty and social meaning. Or, to take another example, an old earthenware bowl, admired for its simplicity and its ability to evoke memories of ancient crafts, such as is used in a Japanese tea ceremony, embodies a unique understanding of things. It is hard to picture a tea ceremony around a Styrofoam cup." One might add that this line of thinking also corresponds to the later Heidegger's critique of the *Ge-stell*, the technical enframement through which things, along with the world as such, come to be viewed as mere entities of an omnipresent *Be-stand*, a standing reserve or stockpile, in which everything, having lost the capacity for distance, absence, and singularity, can simply be placed on order—a treacherous affirmation of the modern world's principal orderability. The true heir, by contrast, engages tirelessly with the things that are handed down, undeterred by the omnipresent prejudice that privileges efficiency, instrumentality, usefulness, and convenience over the slow rhythms of relating to one's own world and the world of others and otherness.

102

Debts. — What does one generation owe to another? Does inheritance indebt one generation to the next — and if so, in what would that debt consist and how would it manifest itself in the intellectual and quotidian aspects of contemporary life? One might say that the epic, six-hour-long play *The Inheritance* by Matthew Lopez, which premiered in London in 2018 and opened in New York City in 2019, is an extended meditation on these questions. A transformative reinterpretation of E. M. Forster's 1910 novel *Howards End*, it explores the lives, political attitudes, and modes of being-in-the-world of gay men in New York in the generation following the one which experienced the peak of the AIDS pandemic. *The Inheritance* stages questions of legacy, indebtedness, and spectral relatedness in ways that remain partially opaque, even as they make contemporary life and its singular *Lebensgefühl* precisely what they are. There can be no inheritance without debt, and that uneasy indebtedness tends to retain its enigmatic character even and especially when facing sustained attempts at being understood.

103

No Debts?—Do children inherit a special debt to their elders, in addition to a series of traits, ways of thinking, speaking, and acting—in short, particular modes of being-in-the-world—and, sometimes, material goods? The idea expressed by the biblical commandment to "Honor thy father and thy mother" would seem to reach far beyond the religious and cultural traditions of the Hebrew Bible in this context. By contrast, in her 2018 book *Warum wir unseren Eltern nichts schulden* (Why we do not owe anything to our parents), the Swiss philosopher Barbara Bleisch sets out to develop arguments in favor of the notion that there is no special responsibility that children have to their parents—in short, that there is no such thing as filial duty. Upon closer inspection, however, it turns out that she does not quite mean it. One might helpfully recall a German idiom here: Es wird nichts so heiß gegessen, wie es gekocht wird ("Nothing is eaten as hot as it is cooked").

104

Parental Riddles. — Whatever else may be said about him or her, the inheritor is always also fundamentally an heir to the legacy inscribed in him or her by the parents. In whatever relation heirs may stand to their father and mother, the inheritor's being-in-the-world is inflected in significant ways by the terms of that particular heritage, complex and overdetermined as it may be. Yet within that heritage, there may well be asymmetry and aberration. *Ecce Home: How One Becomes What One Is*, composed by Nietzsche in a burst of creative ecstasy in the span of only a few weeks in late 1888, expresses the "uniqueness" of his existence "in the form of a riddle": "As my father I have already died, as my mother I still live and grow old." It is as if part of the fragmented Nietzschean heir-self survived precisely in the realization that something else within him had ceased to be; the heir-self lives on precisely to the extent that it is also no longer fully alive as an integral whole, that is, as a self-identical structure of ipseity ruled by a sovereign consciousness. In order to appreciate this observation, it is perhaps helpful to know that Nietzsche had a much closer relationship with his father, who died young, than he did with his mother, who outlived Nietzsche's father by a significant number of years. Yet what is crucial here is the structural way in which Nietzsche's narrative portrays the survival of part of himself (in this case, a maternal element) in terms of a simultaneous non-survival (here, a paternal element), so that what emerges is the rhetorical image of an inheriting self both dead and alive, partially deceased and partially living on. It is such a fragmented heir-self that receives its legacy and that propels the narrative of its troubled origins into presence:

"The ice is near, the solitude is terrible—but how peacefully all things lie in the light! how freely one breathes! how much one feels *beneath* one!—Philosophy, as I have hitherto understood and lived it, is a voluntary living in ice and high mountains—a seeking after everything strange and questionable in existence." And it is precisely from the vantage point of this strange and questionable life that Nietzsche's narrative issues forth: "And so I tell myself my life" ("Und so erzähle ich mir mein Leben"). This telling of a life to one's heir-self is a primordial act of inheriting.

105

Mothers of the Heir. — For heirs, the act of inheriting from parents — that is, of confronting the legacy that has made them who they are in decisive ways — is suffused with a simultaneous recognition of parental aberration. In light of Nietzsche's exceedingly complex relationship with his mother, one may hear a latter-day Nietzschean perspective articulated in Marguerite Duras's apodictic statement: "Our mothers always remain the strangest, craziest people we've ever met." (One should not fail to concede that, spoken by true heirs, this statement may also be a compliment, among other things.)

106

Children of the Heir. — There is a kind of anticipated legacy of the self that gives vigilant heirs pause. Such consideration makes manifest the heirs' concern not only with what they themselves inherit, but also with what they, as receiving heirs and potential bequeathers, are likely to hand down to those who follow them. Heirs may well see themselves as the testators of a legacy that they could not fully endorse if it were to come about—perhaps especially as regards the heirs' own children as heirs. In a long letter from June 1916, Kafka writes to Felice Bauer, the woman to whom he was twice engaged but whom he never married:

> Now consider, Felice, the change that marriage would bring about for us, what each would lose and each would gain. I should lose my (for the most part) terrible loneliness, and you, whom I love above all others, would be my gain. Whereas you would lose the life you have lived hitherto, with which you were almost completely satisfied. You would lose Berlin, the office you enjoy, your girl friends, the small pleasures of life, the prospect of marrying a decent, cheerful, healthy man, of having beautiful, healthy children for whom, if you think about it, you clearly long. In place of these incalculable losses, you would gain a sick, weak, unsociable, taciturn, gloomy, stiff, almost hopeless man who possibly has but one virtue, which is that he loves you. Instead of sacrificing yourself for real children, which would be in accordance with your nature as a healthy girl, you would have to sacrifice yourself for this man who is childish, but childish in the worst sense, and who at best might learn from you, letter by letter, the ways of human speech.

Kafka's sentences encrypt not only his deep ambivalence toward marriage but, indeed, toward "life." At the same time, they bespeak a radical guardedness toward the idea of handing down to his potential children—and, for that matter, to his potential wife—an inheritance of misfortune, misery, unhappiness, and aberration. Kafka resists perpetuating the difficult and arduous legacy that has created his own being-in-the-world, which is diagnosed in terms of a monstrous inheritance in his *Brief an den Vater* (*Letter to the Father*) and related documents. Troubled heirs sometimes wish to engender no further heirs themselves.

Fathers (Worrisome Bequeathing). — The thought that one may bequeathe to future generations something that one does not understand oneself can be the cause of persistent worry and anxiety. After all, handing something down to future heirs does not necessarily imply a voluntary act or a thought-out, sovereign procedure over which a consciousness may exercise full control. One way of reading the much-debated ending of Kafka's "Die Sorge des Hausvaters" ("The Worry of the Father of the Family"), in which the narrating voice expands its reflections on the inscrutable and undefinable being named Odradek to include that spool-like being's possible relation to futurity, touches precisely upon the notion of an imagined future inheritance that cannot be contained by this or that stable meaning. As the narrating voice reflects: "I ask myself in vain what will become of him. Can he die? Everything that dies has previously had some sort of goal, some kind of activity, and that activity is what has worn it down; this does not apply to Odradek." The narrator continues the reflection by asking: "And so, can I expect that one day, with his bits of thread trailing behind him, he will come clattering down the stairs, say, at the feet of my children and my grandchildren ["noch vor den Füßen meiner Kinder und Kindeskinder mit nachschweifendem Zwirnsfaden die Treppe hinunterkollern"]? True, he clearly harms no one; but the idea that, on top of everything else, he might outlive me, that idea I find almost painful." The emphasis here at the end of Kafka's story is on the future generations, the heirs to come, who may be confronted with an inheritance that they do not understand. The narrating voice's perpetual care, worry, and concern (*Sorge*) lie not only with its own inability to understand the enigma that is Odradek but also with how this meaning-defying being that traverses the house will be handed down to generations to come, unintentionally foisted upon baffled heirs who will not be able to read Odradek. While the finitude of the narrator-testator is presumed to be unavoidable, Odradek's death is no certainty. In other words, while those who attempt to read for the refractory meaning of Odradek are always already touched by their own future death, the enigma itself may well survive and thus continue to hand itself down the generational chains of reader-heirs. The realization that the phenomenon retreating from meaning may turn out to be the very inheritance involuntarily bequeathed to coming generations is marked by an experience of discomfort, anxiety, even pain. Not only does the unreadable being perpetually confound the narrator's efforts at understanding, it also threatens to outlive him and to become a source of consternation for those who will inherit from the narrator. The question of whether Odradek is capable of dying ("Kann er denn sterben?") remains open and perpetually unanswered, even unanswerable, in Kafka's text—and with it, the question of inheritance itself. What the heirs stand to inherit from the father of the family—the worrying *Hausvater* in whose care they stand—is not this or that stable content, this or that concrete inheritance. What they stand to inherit, rather, is a constellation of anxiety, care, worry, and concern—*die Sorge* itself. Perhaps *die Sorge*, with all the powerful demands that it makes and its perpetual unreadability, is the true object of any substantive inheritance.

Inherited Jouissance. — A psychoanalytic perspective on inheritance allows us to view the phenomenon in terms of an ongoing transmission, that is, as something other than a conscious mental determination or the final shaping of a discrete ego. On the contrary, the transmission is seen as the beginning or activation of an ego that is constantly taking shape, continuing to transform and evolve along paths that are open, always related to others and their particular forms of otherness, and consequently unforeseeable. As the psychoanalytic critic Joan Copjec justly reminds us, psychoanalytic discourse "speaks a lot about the inheritance of something like a culture or ethnicity (think of *Moses and Monotheism,* for example) and thinks the mechanisms of this inheritance other than as an imprinting. Inheritance, Freud says in *The Ego and the Id,* cannot take place solely through the ego (that is, it cannot take place more or less in the way cultural constructionists think it does), but must go through the id." Yet, she continues, what "we inherit through the id, or as *jouissance,* is not something we have conscious access to and it does not mold us; we have to mold or express it." Copjec reminds us that, as a transformative and recalcitrant heir to Freud, Lacan conceptualizes "*jouissance* as a kind of inheritance we can use, but not use up; something that can never be titled to us. By this he means that *jouissance* is not like property (or a property of an individual), but like common property in the Communist sense." As a consequence, it "is not ours alone, even if it is the most intimate part of who we are. What every individual inherits is not an identity or identifying property, but a potentiality, a capacity, which does not prescribe in advance what it is a potential for."

To be hospitable to a proffered inheritance that can be used but not be used up, a legacy that promises incessantly without ever being exhaustible, means engaging with a notion of potentiality that is shared by everyone, even if it seems to belong to no one. Such an inheritance, like *jouissance* itself, is always excessive. It wishes to be pushed forward and transmitted—as a form of ex-pression, of pressing out—without the possibility of containment by a stable ego with sentient access to that inheritance over which it might exercise conscious and sovereign control.

109

Self-Inheritance of Time I. — Inheritance is one of the names for the self-inheritance of time. We inherit our experiences in and as time; it is in the dimension of temporality that we bequeath something to ourselves, even — and especially — something that is rudimentary, inchoate, or that defies our grasp, like an ancient memory. In her melancholic tale *Sommerstück*, the writer Christa Wolf reflects on a summer long ago: "There were times when we wondered how we would once think back upon these years, what we would tell ourselves and others about them. But we did not really believe that our time was limited." And she continues: "Back then, we say today, we lived. When we wonder why that summer, in our memory, appears singular and endless, we have a hard time finding the sober tone that alone is appropriate for the rare appearances to which life exposes us. Most of the time when that summer is brought up between us, we act as though we had it in our hands. But in truth it had us in its hands and did with us as it wished." The experience of time and the narratives we tell ourselves about our experiences in time are inextricably intertwined with the vicissitudinous inheritance of our own experiences. We do not control the memory, meaning, and legacy of these moments in time — we inherit them in the blurry yet passionate way in which we may remember a remarkable summer many years ago, at which time, in our recollection, time did not exist. This legacy of lost time inhabits us as the self-inheritance of time.

110

Self-Inheritance of Time II. — How we inherit ourselves through time is a function of the account we offer of our past as we inherit it today, in the reflective, discursive act of self-inheritance. We attribute meaning to the legacy of our past experiences of which we could not possibly have been aware at the time. Martin Walser, in his autobiographically inflected 1998 novel *Ein springender Brunnen* (*A Gushing Fountain*), puts it well: "As long as something is, it isn't what it will have been. When something is past, you are no longer the person it happened to, but you're closer to him than to others. Although the past did not exist when it was present, it now obtrudes as if it had been as it now presents itself. But as long as something is, it isn't what it will have been." And Walser continues: "When something is past, you are no longer the person it happened to. When things were that we now say used to be, we didn't know they were. Now we say it used to be thus and so, although back when it was, we knew nothing about what we say now." In this sense, the self-inheritance of one's own time is always out of joint, overdetermined by interpretations and delayed elaborations that always exceed, and also fall short of, whatever we consider the "original" experience to have been. To be an heir who inherits him- or herself and his or her own (lost) time is to recognize that both the person to whom, and the time in which, the one-time experience that is to be recalled, explained, and inherited exists today, if it exists at all, only as the phantasm of a haunting absence.

111

Applied Self-Inheritance. — No act of inheriting can be thought in isolation from the notion of bequeathing. Likewise, any inheritor is an actual or potential testator him- or herself. How, then, might an inheritor foresee what it would mean to be a testator even before one's death, that is, to apprehend the experience of bequeathing, of disseminating — or *being* disseminated — while still alive? In this regard, it is instructive to recall a scene from a 1995 conference, held at the University of Luton in the UK, entitled "Applied Derrida." Derrida, who was asked to be present at this conference, listened patiently and, for the most part silently, over a number of days to presentations about him and his work, and later granted an interview to the conference organizers that was published under the title "As If I Were Dead." Reflecting on the question of "application" and the manifold meanings in which the terms applying, applied, application etc. had been construed by various speakers over the course of the event, Derrida offered the surprising hypothesis, condensed into a single sentence: "I am Applied Derrida." Working through the implications of this statement in the context of the conference's theme, Derrida pauses to reflect on the experience of being a quasi-testator who eavesdrops on a discourse that is about him but that does not actually need him — at least not in the sense of his being alive and present. It is as though the bequeather had been granted the unusual experience of listening to others speak about him as if here were absent, or merely an abstract concept. It is as though the testator himself were permitted, if only for a brief moment, to inherit (from) his own inheritors, receiving an inheritance that travels in the other direction, back to him, so to speak. (One might add that the quasi-backward movement of this inheritance corresponds, remarkably, to the earlier English meaning of the verb "to inherit," which is "to bequeath to someone.") Derrida comments upon the experience of the backward inheritance by averring, in impromptu English sentences:

> You can imagine that when one comes to a conference entitled "Applied *You*," you experience the situation in which it is *as if* you were dead. Finally. Now, amongst the reasons why on many occasions I do agree to attend conferences on me is because, after a lot of hesitations, a lot of inner contradictions, I would like to see what it looks like *as if* I were dead, listening to what people are saying, listening and being among them, while not playing the role of the pathetic dead person. If I had declined the invitation I would have played the role of the master or the dead one, the corpse who doesn't come, yet who hounds you. But I wanted to be with you, one amongst the others, listening, and sometimes not understanding what was going on because English is difficult for me. . . . This is an experiment of acting *as if you were dead*. . . . But what does it mean to be dead, when you are not totally dead? It means that you look at things the way they are *as such*, you look at the object *as such*. To perceive the bottle *as such* means to see the bottle as it would be without me. . . .
>
> The older I get, the more I have to ask myself why we are frightened by death, why we are scared, and I suppose that you, as well as I, are scared by death. It's a very strange question, it's very difficult to know why we are scared. On the one hand, we are scared because we think we won't be there anymore. . . . But, on the other hand, what is scarier is the fantasy—and this is the origin of the fear—the fantasy that we are going to be present at . . . this non-world, at our own death. We will continue to be dead, that is, absent, while attending the actual world, being deprived of sharing the life of the survivors. That is even more terrible: dead without being dead. . . .

But at the same time, it is the most reassuring hope we have that, although dead, we will continue to look, to listen to everything, to observe what's going on. What is the difference between . . . the situation of being at an event such as this, and the situation I am describing? It is the situation or quasi-experience in which you are named, called, quoted, referred to, while being absent or keeping silent. So, it's an experiment in quasi-dying, it's a quasi-transcendental death. That is what I am experiencing here, and I am thanking you for that too; and I am sure that you are sharing this experience with me.

The as-if-ness of this kind of quasi-death, in which one hears the discourses of the others who talk about one as if one were already dead subtly exhibits some of the subterranean links between a testator and the heir in the backward movement of inheritance. The one who listens in on discourses by others about him or her becomes the witness to a scene that is normally reserved for situations in which he or she is absent or dead—and to which he or she is therefore unable to bear witness at all. This is how one's name will circulate after one's actual death—at least if it is not forgotten and does not slide out of the world's sphere of attention altogether. After all, in times marked by my absence or death, the others will no longer talk *to* me but only *about* me. There is, one might say, a triple shift: a grammatical shift in prepositions; an ontological shift; and a shift in the discourse's mode of address. A form of self-inheritance, real or imagined, proceeds through this eavesdropping on the others as they evoke, refer to, and discuss the bequeathing self as if it were already dead.

112

Self-Inheritance Tripped Up. — There is a form of self-inheritance that causes the heir — in this case, a self-heir or self-inheritor — to trip. What the heir has bequeathed to him- or herself may have developed in unexpected ways that are incommensurate with the intentions laid down in the original testament or inheritance plan as initially envisioned. As Goethe puts it in his *Maxims and Reflections*: "I stumbled over the roots of the tree I had myself planted" ("Ich bin über die Wurzeln des Baumes gestolpert, den ich gepflanzt hatte").

113

Perverse Inheritance. — The possibility of perversion is always already inscribed in every act of inheriting. In such cases, the heir may — whether intentionally or not — abuse a legacy in order to foster his or her own agenda in the name of the testator. In a 1931 article for the journal *Die Literarische Welt*, entitled "Nietzsche und das Archiv seiner Schwester" ("Nietzsche and the Archive of His Sister"), Benjamin reflects on the peculiar inheritance that Elisabeth Förster-Nietzsche performs in the context of the Weimar Nietzsche Archive, which she helped to establish. He recalls a story first told by Baron Friedrich von Schennis. At a dinner party celebrating one of Nietzsche's last birthdays, guests were invited to sit at a long table on the upper floor of the house in Weimar where Nietzsche resided. Near the head of the dinner table a podium was cordoned off from the rest of the room by a purple curtain. As the dinner was coming to a close, the curtain was ceremoniously pulled open, and the guests were presented with a mentally ill and physically deteriorated Nietzsche sitting in an armchair, dressed in a toga-like outfit, slightly drooling, and staring blankly into space. This frightening and shameful tableau, Benjamin suggests, could be seen as embodying one of the trajectories of Nietzsche's intellectual inheritance. Benjamin is critical of the way in which Nietzsche's sister "assumed the thinker's inheritance" ("das Erbe des Denkers antrat"), which ironically serves to undermine the ideas of the very one whom it claims to honor. Benjamin explains that "there is an abyss" ("denn es sind Abgründe") between Nietzsche's complex legacy and the modes of inheriting — suffused with nationalistic, anti-Semitic, and even proto-fascist ideological strands — that monopolized the minds of certain self-proclaimed heirs of Nietzsche at the time. In some sense, those who were in charge of the Archive at the time may be said to have failed in their roles as heirs of Nietzsche's intellectual legacy not only because they mobilized Nietzsche for the advancement of their own personal agendas, but also because they failed to take seriously the demand for a ceaseless, restless, interminable interpretation that Nietzsche's textual figures impose on his heirs. These heirs failed to grasp the idea that Benjamin advances in a 1923 letter to his friend Florens Christian Rang, that "all human knowledge, if it is meant to be able to justify itself, must take on no other form than that of interpretation." This mode of emphatic interpretation lies at the heart of any genuine, unpredictable, and irreducibly non-self-identical act of intellectual inheritance.

114

Unreasonable Reason. — Inheriting the legacy of what is called reason also means to inherit the insight that reason can be instrumentalized in such a narrowly reasonable way as to become utterly *unreasonable*. The heritage of this vexing problem is lodged at the core of the story that Horkheimer and Adorno attempt to narrate in *Dialectic of Enlightenment* (1944), beginning with the disenchantment of Odysseus, through the historical Enlightenment (*Aufklärung*), to the siblings named fascism and capitalism.

115

Faulty Origins. — Circumspect heirs must be mindful that whatever they inherit may be tainted by a fault in its origin. In his 1970 reexamination of Husserl's concept of the *Lebenswelt*, or world of lived experience, the philosopher David Carr, an American scholar and translator of Husserl, points to the threat posed by the inheritance of potentially faulty origins. He remarks that "philosophy, as Husserl recognized and insisted at the end of his life, is like any other cultural activity in existing as a cumulative *tradition*; that is, it is able to proceed by being able to take its origins and its fundamental task for granted; it owes its on-going mode of being to its capacity to move away from and in a certain sense forget its origins." But, Carr argues, "in exchange for this very capacity to move forward, it always runs the risk of not only forgetting but also being unable to reactivate and critically examine its origins. And if the origins are faulty, the heirs to the tradition may inherit such faults through too little critical awareness of what they owe to the past." Heirs must remain vigilant not only with regard to the occlusion or disarticulation of origin that may have propelled them forward, but also with respect to the possibility that a faultiness inscribed in the very cracks of that origin (its *Ur-sprung*, literally its primal leap or fissure) may work against their efforts at critical understanding. To inherit therefore always also requires of the heirs a sustained examination of the status — and indeed the very concept — of origin itself.

116

Heirs of the Ages. — In late modernity, the inheritance of progress can no longer be taken for granted. To view the legacy of the idea of progress in a dialectical manner—both as a liberatory potentiality and as form of tacit enslavement—the heir must learn to inherit the idea of progress differently. Critical moments in Kant's transcendental idealism already challenge the notion of unquestionable linear progress. In the twentieth and twenty-first centuries, the legacy of great destructions—from fully technologized World Wars to state-sponsored industrial genocide, environmental devastation and techno-capitalist forms of exploitation—the "age of progress" hands itself down in differently modulated terms. In the brief reflection he chose to entitle "The Heirs of the Ages" and which he subsequently included in his 1933 collection *Mein Weltbild*, Einstein warns: "Previous generations were able to look upon intellectual and cultural progress as simply the inherited fruits of their forebears' labours, which made life easier and more beautiful for them. But the calamities of our times show us that this was a fatal illusion. We see now that the greatest efforts are needed if this legacy of humanity's is to prove a blessing and not a curse." Einstein's plea to be an heir not only of one age but of many—that is, not only *of* but *for* the ages—calls upon us to confront the illusion of undialectical progress with an eye toward that, within the postulates of alleged progress, which may already be silently working to oppose, even to undo, what this progress claims, on the surface, to accomplish. This legacy of progress requires the heirs of the ages to be vigilant not only as regards the progress it appears to offer them, but also with respect to its—typically occluded—dark underbelly.

117

Inheriting the Sound of Silence I. — When it comes to an intellectual legacy, the heir inherits not only discourse but also silence. Attempting to do justice to what has not been said fully as much as what has, the heir must be mindful of the possibility that these two aspects of the inheritance cannot reliably be told apart—and, in fact, do not necessarily preclude each other. For Foucault in *The History of Sexuality*, "silence itself—the things one declines to say, or is forbidden to name" is "less the absolute limit of discourse, the other side from which it is separated by a strict boundary, than an element that functions alongside the things said, with them and in relation to them." Therefore, there "is no binary division to be made between what one says and what one does not say; we must try to determine the different ways of not saying such things, how those who can and those who cannot speak of them are distributed, which type of discourse is authorized, or which form of discretion is required in either case." As a result, there is "not one but many silences, and they are an integral part of the strategies that underlie and permeate discourses." If silence and discourse do not stand in a binary opposition to each other, and silence is but a function and a symptom of discursivity, the heir who wishes—or is summoned—to inherit these two modes must exercise a critical vigilance and attunement to their manifold imbrications. To inherit a form of silence or the unsaid is always also a form of inheriting discourse itself, and the reverse is true as well. Making sense of the infinite entwinement of the said and the unsaid that precedes them and continuously haunts them during the act of inheriting is the reader-heirs' legacy.

Inheriting the Sound of Silence II.—What sort of bequest could silence have yet in store for us? Is the silence that itself is split in manifold ways still inheritable as silence today? Or does the disposition of its testimony bar it from an appropriation that would differentiate itself into parts, take its distance, and inscribe itself into new contexts? Are the legacies of the silent orphaned? In his Svendborg poem from the late 1930s, "An die Nachgeborenen" ("To Those Born Later" or "To Those Who Follow in Our Wake"), Brecht paradigmatically sets the scene for reflecting upon silence as follows: "What times are these when / A conversation about trees is nearly a crime / Because it encloses so many unspeakable deeds in silence?" ("Was sind das für Zeiten, wo / Ein Gespräch *über* Bäume fast ein Verbrechen ist / Weil es ein Schweigen *über* so viele Untaten einschließt?"). The times that beset the lyrical self and pose such grave difficulties for speaking are, first and foremost, those of German fascism and its state-sponsored program of genocide. Today, the times that make a conversation about trees nearly a crime might include expansion-enthralled globalization, ideologized techno-capitalism, financial imperialism, unfettered profit fetishism, and a radically instrumentalized exploitation of the environment that has led to a worldwide climate crisis. Brecht emphasizes not only the question of how to justify speaking of seemingly trivial, everyday things such as trees in dark times, but also what it might mean to engage with the question of inheriting a certain form of neglect. In this case, speaking of such subjects entails ethical and political misconduct. By failing to confront more dire matters, one tacitly assents to them—through omission—in silence. What kind of an inheritance takes place here? At another level, one could perhaps speak of euphemism with regard to the silence that can be discerned in a conversation about trees, especially if one conceives of this concept, with Agamben, in terms of its proper Greek provenance as *euphemein*, or "adoring in silence." The moment of this devotional silence itself contributes, even if unintentionally, to the perpetuation of the silenced horrors. Brecht's trees also stand for the legacy of a certain aestheticism, which self-satisfiedly turns away from worldly or overtly political matters, and for the entertainment branch of the consciousness-industry that incites entire countries to "seek the next superstar" (to echo the title of a popular German TV show), while others, in supposedly distant quarters of the globe, are oppressed, exploited, and murdered in the name of the business interests of those same media-crazed countries. What times are these, as we might reformulate Brecht's verses today, in which it is nearly a crime to converse about the latest "achievements" of civilization, such as the perhaps ironically dubbed "smart phone," which may well outrank, on the cultural admiration scale, the first "smart bombs" the United States dropped over Iraq in the beginning of the 1990s, or to discuss the hairstyles and voices of participants in expensively produced and propagated casting shows—because it implies silence about so many horrible things.

From the perspective of the history of philosophy, however, one might add that the heritage of Brecht's lyrical conversation on silence is just as much a legacy of Marx's eleventh thesis on Feuerbach, which states that "the philosophers have only *interpreted* the world in various ways; the point, however, is to *change* it." If philosophical thinking remains, even when it performs the gestures of materialism, arrested in pure and silent reflection, it can generate no impulse towards change. Merely a descriptive, repetitive, and ultimately silent thought-process, it would remain a performance of confirmation. Likewise, if the conversation about trees endures in pure self-referentiality—as one could interpret Brecht through Marx—striving toward no change in the status quo, then its interpretations would be affirmative, oddly silent. In truth, however, no relation of binary opposition prevails between interpretation and change, since every wish for change must rest upon a previous interpretation that explicates the status quo in an ever yet-to-be-determined way and that permits a corresponding change to come into view. Therefore, with respect to the conversation about trees, there can be no change without interpretation. At the same time, however, the following inversion must be considered, too: there can be no interpretation without change, if only in the realm of consciousness, as it is transformed through interpretive insight. Even the very sentence that appears to place the prevalence of philosophical interpretation in question demands to be lifted out of silence and inherited as it partakes of the interpretive change in the consciousness that explicates it.

Insofar as silence and speech do not stand exclusively in a binary opposition to each other in Brecht's poem, the complex interweaving of theses modes becomes the object of a refractory inheritance. It is in this sense, too, that one might recall Celan's complex inheritance of Brecht, as he responds to Brecht with a poem of his own that precisely performs the inversion of the relationship between silence and speech: "A LEAF, treeless // for Bertolt Brecht: // What times are these / when a conversation / is nearly a crime / because it includes so much / that's already been said?" As Celan's poem addressed to Brecht testifies, silence and speech, rather than mere opposites, are always already imbricated with each other through the logic of mutual supplementarity, especially when it comes to the legacy of guilt and the inheritance of crimes.

119

Fibers. — Inheritance is the name of a future that constitutes itself from the genealogical fibers of what has come to pass. It is the thinking of futurity as such.

120

Inheriting a Question Mark. —Inheriting in the emphatic sense would mean to inherit not a period but a question mark. The main revision that Freud made between the original 1930 publication of *Civilization and Its Discontents* and its second edition in 1931 consisted in adding one more sentence to the end of the book. At first sight, this may not seem like much of a revision, but the effects of this change turn out to be rather dramatic. In wishing to reflect on the "fateful question for the human species," namely, "whether and to what extent their cultural development will succeed in mastering the disturbance of their communal life by the human instinct of aggression and self-destruction," Freud has the original version of the text end with the following declarative sentence: "And now it is to be expected that the other of the two 'Heavenly Powers,' eternal Eros, will make an effort to assert himself in the struggle with his equally immortal adversary." Here, the book ends with a period. Yet one year later, Freud adds the following question after the final sentence: "But who can foresee with what success and with what result?" Now, in the second edition, the book no longer ends with a period but with a question mark. The question mark signals an ending after the end, another ending that renders the end something other than itself. The ending simultaneously calls itself into question as an ending, becoming also a beginning—another beginning. A question mark bespeaks something other than an end or a mere cessation, because it actively elicits a response, even when the question to which the question mark belongs is posed in a rhetorical mode. If the two "immortal" forces, Eros and Thanatos—the affirmative, erotic drive that causes us to bond and to form close-knit groups, and the drive that leads us eternally to destroy, kill, and undo—are what humans and their cultures inherit, this unruly inheritance is one of unsettlance, unease, and anxiety, the Freudian *Angst*. To the extent that a question mark replaces a period as the final sign of Freud's text, the radical uncertainty of this explosive and immortal inheritance is cast into sharp relief. While in the first version there is a sense in which Eros might well rise to the occasion and, through his erotic affirmation and community-building force, keep the violent and powerful destruction wreaked by Thanatos in check, in the second edition such a hopeful note is markedly absent. The question with which that edition ends resonates with echoes of doubtfulness, uncertainty, perhaps even despair. From a historico-political perspective, one might say that Freud must have become increasingly aware, between 1930 and 1931, of the threat that Hitler and Nazi Fascism were coming to pose ever more forcefully. The fact that Hitler was elected Chancellor only two years after the second edition of Freud's book—and its fateful question mark—appeared certainly bore out his uneasy premonition. And yet Freud's question mark is by no means limited in its applicability to the rise of Nazi Fascism and the state-sponsored industrial killing it would perpetrate. It touches, rather, upon a larger struggle within the inheritance and legacy of the human psyche itself, in which our instinctual attraction to committing violence and to visiting destruction upon others and the world is in constant and, for Freud, "immortal" battle with the love of affirmation, preservation, and survival. One might say that any act of inheriting is inflected by this struggle, as is any culture of heirs that finds itself facing urgent questions pertaining to institutions, practices, beliefs, and values—in short, modes of being in the world. Such inheritance can hardly find an end point in a period, or what in British English is called a "full stop." When it comes to the uncertain and unpredictable act of inheriting, there is no full stop, not even a partial stopping—but only and always just a question mark.

121

Not for Cowards. — Being an heir is not for cowards.

122

Weight of the World. — In Peter Handke's *Das Gewicht der Welt* (*The Weight of the World*), one reads: "A fine thing: suddenly to forget about one's history, one's past, to stop feeling that one's present happiness is endangered by what one used to be." To the extent that heirs must incessantly worry about the heritage of their past — which is always also to say: the past of someone else, of others, and of the self *among* these others — they are unlikely to experience such liberatory forgetting. To be sure, heirs do not wallow in the inheritance of their history in the way that melancholics do; yet the heirs' meditative, interpretative vigilance does not allow them to disengage from the genealogies that have made the heirs who they are and made their thoughts what they are. Can heirs ever get out from under the weight of the world?

123

Making Treasures Speak. — The process of inheriting a transformative and challenging cultural legacy reveals that what is handed down to the heir differs radically from what the heir expected to find there. As Hannah Arendt remarks in the context of her reflections on the occasion of the eightieth birthday of her former teacher Heidegger: "The cultural treasures of the past, believed to be dead, are being made to speak, in the course of which it turns out that they propose things altogether different than what had been thought." By allowing cultural and intellectual treasures of the past to speak, the heir not only rescues them from oblivion but also allows them to speak on the far side of any received wisdom about them, that is, as *themselves* and thus *differently*. The responsible heir emerges as the conduit of the irreducible difference — and self-difference — that inflect the past's otherwise mute treasures.

124

Loss.—As much as the heir is concerned with protecting, preserving, maintaining, affirming, and reinscribing, he or she is always acutely aware of the shadow cast by the dialectical other: loss, disappearance, forgetting, erasure, vanishing. In fact, there could be no emphatic act of inheriting at all if it did not also always have to engage with the simultaneous possibility of non-transmission, interruption, failed inheritance, in short: radical and irrecuperable loss. After all, it is not only the case that wherever there is life, there is inheritance; it is also the case that wherever there is life, there is loss. If to live means to experience both inheritance and loss, the complex and shifting relation between the two is never far from an heir's mind. The contemporary German writer Judith Schalansky meditates upon, and follows the intricate paths of, various instances of loss in her recent *Verzeichnis einiger Verluste* (*Register of Some Losses*). On the far side of nostalgia and the longing for impossible recuperation, her text brings into a narrative constellation a number of diverse instances of radical loss—from the Caspian tiger to certain architectural ruins, from the remote equatorial island of Tuanaki that has sunk into nothingness to a painting by Caspar David Friedrich that was consumed by flames, from the lost first film (1919) of German silent-film director F. W. Murnau to the seven vanished books of Mani—by affirming each loss through meticulous description and speculative reflection. As the thought-provoking tales of irrevocable loss united in her book testify, "at bottom every thing is always already rubbish, every building already ruin, and all creating nothing but destruction, including the work of all those disciplines and institutions that proudly proclaim to be preservers of humanity's legacy." The mourning that one feels is directed at "what is gone, what is being missed—of which some relic, a tale, sometimes hardly more than a rumor, a half-erased trace, the reverberation of an echo may have reached us." Here, what emerges is the insight that "earth itself is . . . a rubble heap of past futures, and humanity a randomly assembled, quarrelling community of heirs [sich streitende Erbengemeinschaft] of a numinous pre-time that must be perpetually appropriated and redesigned, dismissed and destroyed, ignored and repressed," with the result that "it is not the future, as is commonly assumed, that presents the true space of possibility, but rather the past." One might say that to inherit is not only a gesture aimed at preventing loss; it also *affirms* loss as such, loss *as* loss. The potentiality and open-endedness of inheritance remind the heir in the most primordial sense that there is passing, that there is decay, *that there is loss.*

125

Generalized Capitalism. — For heirs, making history always also requires a political engagement with the forms of being that the dominant, even hegemonic, paradigms of social and ideological organization consider archaic and therefore tacitly superfluous at any given historical moment. In a dialogue with Bruno Bosteels, Alain Badiou states: "I am surprised to see that today everything that does not amount to surrender pure and simple to generalized capitalism, let us call it thus, is considered to be archaic or old-fashioned, as though in a way there existed no other definition of what it means to be modern than, quite simply, to be at all times caught in the dominant forms of the moment." According to this political diagnosis of our contemporary world and the dominant forms of being that it valorizes, there is a certain short-circuiting at work that mistakes any refusal to accept — and to submit to — the hegemonic and mainstream ideologies that have been imposed surreptitiously onto consciousness for an outmoded, outdated, and essentially obsolete way of inhabiting the world. While during former historical epochs such as the Middle Ages whatever presented itself as new and of the moment tended to be viewed with skepticism and was subjected to the burden of proof to show that it was in fact an improvement over the old, in modernity — and to an unprecedented degree in our own situation of late, neoliberal techno-capitalism — this relation is reversed. Whenever something ostensibly new is introduced, it is the supposedly old or at least that which is already in existence that must prove its continued right to exist, because it is naively assumed that whatever is presented as new is automatically and without further reflection endowed with a superior claim on our collective endorsement. This political mechanism leads to a cultural and ideological situation in which we are expected "to be at all times caught in the dominant forms of the moment," lest we be considered "archaic" and superfluous. By contrast, the responsible, vigilant heirs refuse to be caught up in any dominant forms of this or that moment, not because they are somehow intransigent or closed off to the idea of change, but rather because they understand true change only too well. They recognize whatever appears as contemporary precisely as something that has an invisible history, something contingent that therefore could have been entirely different, a political legacy that comes to the heirs and their fellow inheritors only as an incompletely understood and insufficiently examined inheritance from the past. As such, true heirs are not model citizens of generalized capitalism. They refuse to yield to its unrelenting demands for absolute submission to the ideological paradigm it markets—and strictly enforces—as the supposed necessity of the present moment and its political economy.

126

Nostalgia for the Future.—Receiving an intellectual legacy demands that the heir be sensitively attuned to both the future and the past in such a way as to intensify the experience of a refractory and enigmatic now, that is, the ongoing act of inheriting. In the entry "The 1970s" of his book *Winter*, Norwegian writer Karl Ove Knausgaard has the narrator reflect on his salient attachment to the decade of his childhood and the ways in which his children cannot relate to what appears to them as strange and obscure. He observes: "The longing for the 70s is nothing other than a longing for the future, for back then it existed, people knew that everything would change, but it doesn't exist any longer now that everything has changed." And he adds: "I think all cultural epochs are characterized by these two modes, the existence of a future and the absence of a future, and the strange thing is that culture seems to strive towards the absence of future, as if that were its highest form, when all longings have been fulfilled, but it isn't, because then longing turns towards the past, or towards something else that has been lost or was never accomplished." From the particular vantage point of our thinking of inheritance, we may say that if heirs are possessed of any longing, it is always a longing for both the past (from which their intellectual inheritance stems) and the future (a time to come in which their engagement with that inheritance can be expected to bear fruit). Although the specters of time prevent heirs from being present to themselves in any straightforward manner, the forms of the present that they experience in the act of inheriting are always other-directed—pointing toward the existence of a future (based on an accomplished inheritance), the absence of a future (threatened by the failure to inherit), the legibility of a past (as it may emerge in the rigorous act of reading-inheriting), and the absence of a past (a time gone by that cannot be retrieved owing to a failed attempt to inherit was it has to offer). If heirs are ever struck by nostalgia, it is nostalgia for the future.

127

Rich Inner Life. — Even though true heirs are other-directed, refusing to live solipsistically in their own head, they do have an unusually rich inner life. While they cannot be reduced to their interiority, they engage the full range of human emotion as they ponder the challenging modes of inheritance that traverse their world. In this way, the heirs counter today's dominant affective paradigm, which is characterized by flatness, emotional resignation, and self-absorbed indifference. As early as the 1980s, Fredric Jameson diagnoses the postmodern condition in part as a "cultural pathology" in which there is a noticeable "waning of affect" and in which the uncanny "liberation from anxiety" is simultaneously "a liberation from every other kind of feeling as well." To the extent that the postmodern is not "utterly devoid of feeling," it "may be better and more accurate" to call such remnants of feeling, "following J. F. Lyotard, 'intensities,'" which are merely "free-floating and impersonal." One may say that, by contrast, emphatic heirs are never "liberated" from anxiety or, for that matter, from any other kind of emotion that inhabit their rich inner life. Rather, they engage with the world reflectively, attuned to both the cognitive and the affective demands of an inheritance and those of a world in which that inheritance comes to pass.

128

Doxa. — The emphatic heir embodies an otherness to the two dominant forms of inhabiting what remains of the public sphere in the West today. These two dominant forms can be profiled as follows: On the one side, one finds an angry, resentful, typically nationalist, anti-other, isolationist stance by those who either regard themselves as the losers in an unrelenting global attack on their historical privilege and hegemonic preponderance, that is, the onslaughts of what they regard as undesirable change. On the other side, one finds a dogmatic ideology of self-righteous outrage, laboriously cultivated hypersensitivity, emotional lability, larmoyance stylized as martyrdom in the cause of justice that is paired with an inability to receive criticism, an unshakable and narcissistic belief in having identified the side of what is good, moral, and correct once and for all, a quasi-militant penchant for outlawing points of view that differ from one's own, and the self-infantilizing desire to punish those who hold a different point of view. The true heir, however, cannot be content with either of these uninviting options at the poles of this unfortunate binarism. On the contrary, the heir actively undermines these positions by refusing to yield to their unchallenged doxa, preferring to cultivate reflection, openness, freedom of spirit, and a certain restless vigilance in thinking.

129

Side-Taking. — The legacy of Reinhard Lettau — member of the famed circle of post-World War II German writers named "Gruppe 47" ("Group 47"), which included such literary luminaries as Ingeborg Bachmann, Heinrich Böll, Paul Celan, Hans Magnus Enzensberger, Günter Grass, Peter Handke, Uwe Johnson, Alexander Kluge, Martin Walser, and Peter Weiss, among many others — has somewhat fallen out of public consciousness. Yet Lettau's gestures of thinking and writing remain highly instructive today, especially from the standpoint of coming to terms with the considerable problem of inheritance. Well known for his brilliantly chiseled German prose — which was schooled on the heritage of Kleist and Kafka — he also was famous for his left-wing political interventions and anti-imperialist activism, which at one point caused state authorities to expel him from what was then West Germany. Because of his refusal to accede to received wisdom in any orthodox, predictable, or uncritical manner, Lettau likewise was known for causing consternation not only on the Right, but also on the Left, the side he considered his own. He once expressed his stance as follows: "When everyone is on one side anyway, then it is no mistake to be on the wrong side. I don't have to worry about the one side anymore. But the other side may possibly turn out to be correct" ("Wenn alle sowieso auf einer Seite stehen, ist es kein Fehler, auf der falschen Seite zu sein. Um die eine Seite brauche ich mich nicht mehr zu kümmern. Doch kann die andere unter Umständen richtig sein"). What side, then, does the heir choose, and what side chooses him or her? Is the heir always on the "correct" side, or does he or she sometimes have to pick the "wrong" side in order potentially to emerge as standing up for what is right? The restless, searching heir—who will not allow his or her critical vigilance to be lulled to sleep by the demands made by those who always consider themselves to be on the morally correct side of a world to whose workings they believe themselves to have a more privileged access than the less fortunate—may have a more difficult time than others choosing sides. This does not mean the heir will seek neutrality; he or she is not the Switzerland of thinking. After all, for the heir, the last word has not yet been spoken. As he or she wrestles with the heritage of thinking, his or her inherited being-in-the-world, the heir allows the world to stand before him- or herself in its full complexity, even undecidability—as if suspended between the world of possibilities and a premature taking of sides.

130

Detours and Forest Paths. — There is no map to guide arduously interpreting heirs along the winding roads toward what they wish to learn from their inheritance. No GPS can show them how to arrive — or whether such a location exists at all. The heirs therefore must not be afraid of taking detours, which may provide the way forward for them. One might even say that responsible heirs will embrace the possibility of whatever path they find themselves on, even one that may eventually emerge as a *Holzweg*, "wooden path" or "forest path," that in idiomatic German denotes a movement off the beaten track (especially through the thicket of a forest) that may lead nowhere. And yet, without the permanent risk of inadvertently taking detours and straying off-course into uncharted territory, there can be no genuine act of inheriting. The heirs are the ones who reflect upon the labyrinthine paths of — and thereby opens up to — an existence without roadmaps.

131

Stone. — In his reflections on the philosophical and aesthetic significance of stone, the American philosopher John Sallis engages with the heritage of stone in such variegated contexts as nature, artistic forms including sculpture and dramatic performance, inscriptions on tombstones in Prague's old Jewish cemetery, Ancient Greek temples and Gothic cathedrals, and in forms of humans shelter from the elements. Sallis suggests that Hegel's *Aesthetics* can be read as if it "were an inscription written for the gravestone that would memorialize art, calling it back now that it is dead and gone." "Stone," he adds, "figures prominently in that inscription, especially in what it says of the beginning. Art, recollected in its history, displays its pastness. Most remarkably, it displays that pastness from the beginning, in the stone (that most ancient material) from which art in the beginning shapes much of its work." Inheriting stone would also always mean to inherit the beginning of art, along with its end, which is to say its various ends. Learning to inherit would require the heir to learn to read the inscriptions of stone, in the double sense of this genitive construction.

132

Not Done.—Being an heir means realizing, for better or for worse, that one is far from being done with inheriting. Yet inheriting is hardly an incomplete project in the way that Habermas conceptualizes modernity as an incomplete but, in principle, completable project. Not to be done with inheriting means appreciating its fundamentally incompletable and irreducibly aporetic structure.

Proof. — The heir knows that thinking, including the thinking of inheritance, desires proof. After all, what good is a thought—especially of a propositional kind—that cannot be corroborated by proof? What would be the evidence for its truth-claims if no proof, in whatever form, could be adduced? Nevertheless, there appear to be moments in thinking when the status of proof begins to shift. In an apodictic one-sentence entry in his notebook from 1942, Elias Canetti writes: "Proof is the inherited misfortune of thought" ("Der Beweis ist das Erb-Unglück des Denkens"). If proof can be regarded not only as a strengthening of thought but also as an unwanted misfortune, it is because proof works to close the unending activity of thinking with a finality that belies its principal open-endedness. Proof, when viewed from that perspective, forecloses rather than invites, shuts down consideration instead of perpetuating it. And yet, the burden of proof is inherited along with thinking itself; one may speak of the "Erb-Unglück," the inherited misfortune, of thought precisely to the extent that no legitimate thought could hope to gain acceptance—by others or even by the self that thinks. Is proof sometimes, in more or less tacit or inadvertent ways, the bane of thinking? What is the epistemic relevance of the category of proof when considering the problem of intellectual inheriting? What is the reflective heir's burden of proof?

Creating Concepts. — According to Gilles Deleuze's way of thinking, philosophy can be defined as the creation of concepts. For him, if "philosophy is a discipline that is just as inventive, just as creative as any other discipline," this is because "it consists in creating or inventing concepts." "Concepts," he proceeds to specify, "do not exist ready-made in a kind of heaven waiting for some philosopher to come grab them. Concepts have to be produced. Of course you can't just make them like that. You don't say one day, 'Hey, I am going to invent this concept,' no more than a painter says 'Hey, I am going to make a painting like this' or a filmmaker, 'Hey, I'm going to make this film!'" For Deleuze, there "has to be a necessity, in philosophy and elsewhere; otherwise there is nothing. A creator is not a preacher working for the fun of it. A creator only does what he or she absolutely needs to do. It remains to be said that this necessity, which is a very complex thing, if it exists — means that a philosopher . . . proposes to invent, to create concepts." While the reflective heir is not identical to the philosopher, they share an abiding, thoughtful engagement with concepts and ideas. But the reach of the heir's intellectual activity is not exhausted by invention alone; what the heir stands to inherit comes from a past, a former elsewhere that precedes him or her and his or her acts of inheriting. The heir is propelled by the engagement with what precedes him or her, the interpretation of multiple intellectual and cultural legacies to invent specific ways of thinking, speaking, and writing about these legacies — in dialogue with existing concepts that address *how* to read and receive the concepts that are handed down. While the heir shares a certain conceptual inventiveness with the Deleuzian figure of the philosopher, the heir is distinct insofar as what makes him or her who and what he or she is resides in a sustained tension between the act of receiving and the act of inventing the rules and procedures of that reception. Working incessantly to open up to a heritage that he or she did not invent, the heir invents concepts that would respond to the question of just *how* to open up to the ideas and concepts that inflect this heritage.

135

Those Days. — Sensitively attuned to the remembrance, experience, and temporality of what precedes him or her, the true heir is conscious of his or her own situatedness in time, that is, the process of his or her own aging. As a result, the heir relates differently to different acts of inheritance, depending on the moment in his or her own life trajectory when they occur. The ways in which the heir inherits a legacy as a child or youth differ from the ways in which he or she inherits, for instance, as a middle-aged person or during the later stages of being-in-the-world. In his *Gedankenbuch*, literally "thought-book" or "thinking-book," the contemporary German writer Botho Strauß reflects on a particular phenomenon of recollected experience that also is of epistemic relevance to the figure of the heir:

> My child will remember these days in a blessed manner, which is to say: for it, they will one day become *those days*. As for me, I will not have enough time left for that. Besides, only what one experiences in the process of one's becoming can become the object of transfiguration. Whatever one picks up during one's decline can, however deeply it reaches, become unforgettable at best, but never legendary. Neither my first computer nor my first SMS will ever cross the border of *illo tempore*.
>
> Therefore, the beautiful things one experiences or does during the later stages of one's life are so raw and bare: because the aura of late remembrance remains denied to them. And because one knows this. Every stage of life is like a larva from which a naked, helpless being hatches. From the thick cocoon of cleverness, pain, knowledge, skepticism, and disappointment emerges in the end: the new child. But the time that it needs to recollect its childhood is denied to it.

The salience, transfigurability, and assumed significance of a past experience is tied to the moment in which that experience occurred in the trajectory of a life. In other words, the significance it is granted in our consciousness cannot be thought in isolation from its ability to become, from the viewpoint of many years, even decades in the future, a momentous and existence-shaping event. Imbricated in the process of a person's becoming, these early formative experiences shape the consciousness to such an extent that they become the object of retroactive and belated remembrance, recollection, commemoration, and, on occasion, even life-long mourning. The heir, if he or she wishes to appreciate this constellation, must work to become cognizant of the temporally situated framework that a particular age in the course of an heir's life imposes upon the interpretation of his or her inheritance. To be sure, an emphatic experience of inheriting may shape the heir in a decisive way at any point in life. But only those acts of inheriting that come with their own retroactive capaciousness for belated remembrance can serve as vessels for the preservation and unfolding of the particular "childhood" that comes into existence with each new experience of an act of inheritance.

136

Untimeliness.—Although acutely aware of time and the imbrication of their work with temporality, heirs do not always fully fit into the context of their own times. Grappling with the considerable demands of what has been handed down to them and of what they, in turn, are expected to hand down, heirs may seem to be something other than mere contemporaries to those around them, figures that are too early or too late, inhabiting a temporality that is not quite identical to itself. Heirs find it impossible to be fully contemporary to anyone else, because the inheritance of time makes different demands on everyone. In their struggle to relate to their bequest through the vagaries of time, heirs at times fall out of their times. Skeptical of contemporaneity, they feel closer to the disruptions of time that we have inherited in bequests such as Nietzsche's concept of untimeliness (*das Unzeitgemäße*) and Ernst Bloch's idea of nonsimultaneity, as it is developed in *Erbschaft dieser Zeit* (translated as *The Heritage of Our Times*).

137

Heir to Come. — True heirs are not primarily concerned with ascertaining, defining, and defending once and for all who and what they are. Rather, heirs become reflective witnesses to their own change as they engage in creative acts of inheritance and are transformed by them. Heirs share Foucault's view on keeping the identity of a thinking self suspended. In a 1982 conversation with Rux Martin during his visit at the University of Vermont, Foucault states: "I don't feel that it is necessary to know exactly what I am. The main interest in life and work is to become someone else that you were not in the beginning. . . . The game is worthwhile insofar as we don't know what will be the end." Heirs, too, eschew the quest for stable self-definition in virtue of a reflective engagement with the ways in which the sustained acts of inheriting rework, refashion, and even reinvent the heirs as thinking beings who do not know how their engagements with various legacies will end. The heir knows that, in a certain sense, he or she does not yet exist but, rather, is always still to come. In the end, the true heir will have been *someone else*.

138

Different Heir-Selves.—The heir looks at—and speaks of—him- or herself in variegated ways. The selves that emerge throughout these various acts of inheritance differ from one another, sometimes dramatically. No one sovereign, stable, or self-present consciousness emerges as the heir is called into diverse subject positions depending on the singular demands of a particular inheritance. As Montaigne puts it in the *Essais*, "If I speak of myself in different ways, that is because I look at myself in different ways" ("Si je parle diversement de moi, c'est que je me regarde diversement"). The heir is an heir-function that gives rise to shifting constellations of heir-selves that each require their own singular narrative.

139

Possible Failures. — The emphatic heir affirms the possibility of his or her failure at inheriting, not only as a mere threat, but also as a permanent prospect. The possibility of failing at this task is also the condition of possibility for any responsible act of slow, laborious reading-inheriting. If, for Arendt, true thinking is a "thinking without a banister," one might say that true inheriting is, for the responsible heir, an inheriting without a banister. The heir could tip over at any point.

140

Partial Inheritance. — Heirs do not inherit a past as such. Rather, if they inherit anything at all, they receive only those elements of a past — understood as a former effect of presence — that will not remain themselves. These elements reach into a futurity, a time that is not their own. What heirs inherit is therefore never complete but always partial, non-self-identical, at odds with itself, not exclusively of its own time, but always inscribed in other times that point beyond what is assumed to be its own.

141

No Repetition. — To inherit is not to repeat. It entails, rather, learning how to relate to a legacy in a singular, unprecedented manner. Repetition cannot be the object of a true inheritance, even repetition with a difference.

142

How It Goes. — There is no one way to inherit; no single recipe, no algorithm will address every possible demand that a singular intellectual inheritance can make on the one who receives it. Eschewing all arbitrariness, it is instructive for the heir to recall Brecht's lucid phrase from *Die Dreigroschenoper* (*The Threepenny Opera*): "Es geht auch anders, doch so geht es auch" ("It could also be done differently, but it can be done like this as well").

143

Not for Sale. — True heirs do not submit efficiency reports, nor are their acts of inheriting highly efficient. They have no academic "initiatives" to sell, no pie charts to peddle, no drafts "to workshop." Their ways of inheriting are not "scalable." They do not "shop for classes" during "shopping period." They will neither "cash in" their arguments nor manufacture pre-fabricated "learning outcomes." They will not hawk algorithms to measure "student credit hours" nor triumphantly celebrate "project-based learning" in "hybrid learning environments." They are no "facilitators" of "innovation" in "interactive" or "adaptive" educational "settings," or even in "flipped classrooms." They inherit intellectual legacies that are unlikely to "identify new sources of revenue" to "support the core mission" of this or that institution of higher learning. They are not blindly infatuated with "metrics," and their acts of inheriting may not yield profitable "returns on investment." In short: They reject the current jargon and ideology of the neoliberal managerial academic system that holds today's corporate university in its iron grip. To the true heirs, inheriting an intellectual legacy involves creative acts of reading and interpreting rather than monetizing what remains of the life of the mind. After all, these heirs are heir to a different legacy, the inheritor of other genealogies that, among other things, are not for sale.

144

Wall Street Inherits **Das Kapital.**—Among the remarkable anecdotes that have been handed down to us about Marx and the reception of his work is the following. Although the first official English translation of *Das Kapital* did not sell very well in England, an unauthorized English publication did remarkably well in 1890 in New York City, where its initial run of 5,000 copies sold out rather quickly. The publisher had apparently circulated an announcement among Wall Street bankers that the book includes a description of how capital is accumulated, which turned out to be a great enticement for the financial workers. One wonders how these readers, once they actually perused the text, might have reacted to Marx's scathing critique of capitalism, his analytic denouncement of the enslaving forces of capital and commodity fetishism, or his theory of surplus value in the context of a capitalist exploitation of others' unpaid labor. More is at stake here than a mere act of clever marketing: How a text will be inherited—and possibly read against the grain—cannot be legislated in advance by its testator-author. Intention and reception are not co-extensive within inheritance, even with respect to something as seemingly overdetermined as the Marxian critique of political economy. There can be no receiving of an intellectual inheritance without a perpetual appropriation and reinscription, as the anecdote of Marx on Wall Street reminds us.

145

The Sibling Rivalry of Inherited Space. — In the chapter "Memory and Forgetting" of his *Imagined Communities*, Benedict Anderson points out that, as early as the sixteenth century, Europeans began the rather "strange habit of naming remote places, first in the Americas and Africa, later in Asia, Australia, and Oceania, as 'new' versions of (thereby) 'old' toponyms in their land of origin." Prime examples are toponyms such as New York, Nueva Leon, Nouvelle Orléans, Nova Lisboa, Nieuw Amsterdam, and even Nieuw Zeeland. Anderson's curiosity is sparked not so much by the thought that this naming of spaces of political, geographic, or religious significance "as 'new' was in itself so new," since, after all, in "Southeast Asia, for example, one finds towns of reasonable antiquity whose names also include a term for novelty: Chiangmai (New City), Kotu Bahru (New Town), Pekanbaru (New Market)." Rather, he draws attention to the idea that "in these names 'new' invariably has the meaning of 'successor' to, or 'inheritor' of, something vanished," so that "'new' and 'old' are aligned diachronically, and the former appears always to invoke an ambiguous blessing from the dead." What is "startling," by contrast, "in the American namings of the sixteenth to eighteenth centuries is that 'new' and 'old' were understood synchronically, co-existing within homogenous, empty time." As such, "Vizcaya is there *alongside* Nueva Vizcaya, New London *alongside* London: an idiom of sibling competition rather than of inheritance." Taking up Anderson's observation, one might ask: What is the political toponym that inheritance implies? What is it that the designation "new" in a place name expresses in relation to the act of inheriting? Does the "new" suggest a competitive break with the old or a commemoration of it? Does the topography of the "new" inherit or displace, perpetuate or replace, dislodge or subordinate? To what extent is the space of inheriting always already a form of sibling rivalry? Is not the politics of space and place ultimately a way of relating to the politics of inheriting—and vice versa?

146

Inheriting the Wrong Words. — To have a language, especially a native language, is to be in receipt of an inheritance. One's "own" language always comes from an other, an elsewhere that long predates the self that would claim it as its own. We are thrown into "our" language and its complex history, whether we choose to be thrown or not. What we inherit in that language may not be what we are looking for. While tutoring the handsome Bliznakoff sisters, Vela and Olga, James Joyce sometimes read a few pages from his manuscript of *Ulysses* to them. At times baffled by Joyce's mobilization of foreign words and neologisms, the sisters would ask: "Aren't there enough words for you in English?" And he would reply: "Yes, there are enough, but they aren't the right ones." The inheritance of English could never be enough for Joyce. This is why, in order to supplement the legacy of English, Joyce would travel through Germany, writing down especially noteworthy or untranslatable German words in a special word-diary. This is also why, as his biographer points out, "as early as April 6, 1907, he had threatened to unlearn English to write in French and Italian." To have a language, which is to say, to have inherited a language, is not to have the right words. One's mother tongue cannot be the *alma mater*, the nourishing mother, for all that one seeks in and through language and for all that wishes to be named by us. What matters in language always must first be inherited laboriously from an elsewhere, from another shore, another idiom, another border, another lexicon, another world—in short: from another mother, from one more mother.

147

Creative Solitudes. — If the heir is at home anywhere at all, perhaps the true heir feels most at home, albeit uneasily, in creative solitudes. This does not mean that the heir shuns the world, rejects the company of others, or refuses to engage with the demands of quotidian life. Rather, the acts of inheriting in which the heir engages — and in which he or she is never simply by him- or herself as he or she communicates with the voices of others, including the ghosts of dead others — place him or her in a position of strategic separateness in which his or her creative acts are allowed to come to pass in productive and unforeseeable ways. Reflecting on creative solitudes, the philosopher David Farrell Krell reminds us that no thinker has "ever been able to distinguish" solitude "properly from aloneness or loneliness, even though we know that these states or conditions are far from identical." From this vantage point, creative solitudes do not designate "isolation or self-absorption," or the need to "languish in narcissism, whether dreamily or wretchedly," a way of being that is "not creative but destructive." To be sure, there always is a price to pay for solitude, as any "need for aloneness" is simultaneously a "need to forego something of life" and thus embodies a difficult path to pursue. "Creative solitudes," in other words, "may not have to be mournful, but whenever we are caught up in them we do have to notice that . . . something is in default. Time may seem to stop in such solitudes, but it stops merely in order to gesture toward the transience of things, the very passing of time, the deaths of parents and friends and lovers — along with the demise of ideas, feelings, and sensations — as we write." In order to do justice to the experience of passing in the space of solitude, it is incumbent upon us "to clear a space at the writing table for ghosts, if only because specters too are vulnerable, ephemeral, and, if the ancients are to be believed, wretchedly lonely." Another way to put this is to say that "every creative solitude entertains ghosts" and that we "are always writing with them and for them, even when we are writing against them," so that no "matter how joyous and exhilarating our solitudes may be, they are always haunted," which is a way of realizing that we "may feel at home in them, yet our being-at-home is riddled with uncanny, unhomelike sensations." The heir, too, is conscious of the double nature of his or her creative solitudes—throughout his or her various acts of arduous intellectual inheritance—as a haunted space that also provides the scene of reflection and respite that first make a focused engagement with an intellectual legacy possible.

148

End Times. — To be a true heir is to be mindful of the idea that inheriting itself may well be coming to end—along with the age of the human being as such. In an astute aphorism from 1980, collected in *Das Geheimherz der Uhr* (*The Secret Heart of the Clock*), Canetti reflects: "There is no doubt: the study of man is just beginning, at the same time that his end is in sight." By extension, the same may be said of one of *Homo hereditans'* primal activities, inheriting: The study of inheriting is just beginning, at the same time that its end is in sight. One does not need to be a cultural pessimist to entertain such a possibility.

149

Inheriting Extinction. — There is nothing self-evident about the notion that what and how one inherits will in turn sustain the future of inheriting. On the contrary, what one inherits, even *that* one inherits at all, can no longer be taken for granted in times of ecocide, global warming, lethal worldwide pandemics, and the disastrous effects of what has come to be called the Anthropocene. When viewed from a certain perspective, our current political and ontological moment of worldwide ecological crisis drastically displays the consequences of our species' collective failure to inherit responsibly. We do not appear to have learned to inherit an ecological awareness and praxis that could sustain a collective future to come, a mode of inheriting through which future generations, too, would be permitted to inherit something other than catastrophe. Does climate change, as the agent of a catastrophic future, name the end of inheriting as such — that is, the end times in which time ends — or does it name the ever-belated injunction to inherit differently, sustainably? If any heirs are left — that is, if there should be any heirs in an ecological time that is yet to come — what will they inherit from us, and what will notions such as "world," "earth," "dwelling," or even "life" still mean to them? Is there an other to the inheritance of extinction and to the extinction of all inheritance?

Reference Matter

Citations are provided by thesis number. In cases where no published translation is cited, translations are my own. On occasion, existing translations have been adjusted to enhance their fidelity to the original.

1. This thesis, along with theses 4, 7–9, 11, 14, 18, 20, 24, 25–7, 30, 31, and 33–5, are translated and reworked portions of Chapter 1 in my *Verwaiste Hinterlassenschaften. Formen gespenstischen Erbens* (Berlin: Matthes & Seitz, 2016). Earlier versions of English translations of a few of those theses adapted from *Verwaiste Hinterlassenschaften* first appeared as "He Who Inherits, Interprets: 14 Theses," *MLN*, 133:3 (2018), 472–86.
2. I thank Dimitris Vardoulakis for his thoughts on the positionality of the Greek θέσις.
3. Friedrich Nietzsche, *Anti-Education: On the Future of Our Educational Institutions*, trans. Damion Searls, eds. Paul Reitter and Chad Wellmon (New York: NYRB, 2016), 91, 93.
5. Augustine cited in Josef Pieper, *Überlieferung. Begriff und Anspruch* (Munich: Kösel, 1970), 29.
6. Albert Einstein, *The World As I See It*, trans. Alan Harris (New York: Covici Friede, 1934), 260.
7. Johann Wolfgang Goethe, *Faust, Werke. Hamburger Ausgabe in 14 Bänden*, ed. Erich Trunz (Munich: DTV, 1988), vol. 3, 29. Friedrich Hölderlin, *Sämtliche Werke und Briefe*, ed. Michael Knaupp (Munch: Hanser, 1992), vol. 2, 913.
9. Sigmund Freud, *Totem and Taboo*, trans. James Strachey (New York: Norton, 1989), 196.
10. Martin Heidegger, *Elucidations of Hölderlin's Poetry*, trans. Keith Hoeller (New York: Humanity, 2000), 36.
11. Stefan Willer, Sigrid Weigel, and Bernhard Jussen, "Erbe, Erbschaft, Vererbung," *Erbe. Übertragungskonzepte zwischen Natur und Kultur*, eds. Willer, Weigel, and Jussen (Berlin: Suhrkamp, 2013), 7–36, here 36.
15. Jacques Derrida, "The Deconstruction of Actuality," *Negotiations: Interventions and Interviews, 1971–2001*, trans., ed., and Introduction by Elizabeth Rottenberg (Stanford: Stanford University Press, 2002), 85–116, here 111.
19. Nathaniel Hawthorne, *The American Notebooks*, ed. Randall Stewart (New Haven: Yale University Press, 1932), 130.

20. Karl Marx and Friedrich Engels, *The Communist Manifesto*, trans. Samuel Moore, ed. Martin Malia (New York: Penguin, 1998), 75.

21. Ernst Bloch, *Verfremdungen I* (Frankfurt am Main: Suhrkamp, 1962), 218.

22. Walter Benjamin, "Das Tagebuch," *Gesammelte Schriften*, eds. Rolf Tiedemann and Hermann Schweppenhäuser (Frankfurt am Main: Suhrkamp, 1991), vol. 2, 96–103, here 103.

23. Rainer Maria Rilke, *The Dark Interval: Letters on Loss, Grief, and Transformation*, trans. and ed. Ulrich Baer (New York: Modern Library, 2018), 3.

25. These etymological remarks draw on the entries on "Erbe" in *Duden Etymologie. Herkunftswörterbuch der deutschen Sprache* (Mannheim: Duden, 1963), 141, and *Etymologisches Wörterbuch des Deutschen* (München: DTV, 1998), 292. An earlier version of part of this thesis appeared in my *Inheriting Walter Benjamin* (London: Bloomsbury, 2016) and, in German, in *Verwaiste Hinterlassenschaften*.

27. Gotthold Ephraim Lessing, *Der Schlaftrunk, Das dichterische Werk*, eds. Herbert G. Göpfert and Gerd Hillen (München: DTV, 1979), vol. 2, 519–44, here 524. Thomas Bernhard, *Auslöschung. Ein Zerfall* (Frankfurt am Main: Suhrkamp, 1986), 483.

28. The historical information in this thesis follows P. Wrzecionko, "Erbsünde," in *Historisches Wörterbuch der Philosophie*, ed. Joachim Ritter (Basel: Schwabe, 1972), vol. 2, 604–7. Part of this thesis appeared in an earlier version in my *Inheriting Walter Benjamin*.

29. Friedrich Nietzsche, *Jenseits von Gut und Böse, Kritische Studienausgabe*, eds. Giorgio Colli and Mazzino Montinari (Munich and Berlin: DTV and DeGruyter, 1999), vol. 5, 98.

31. Georg Wilhelm Friedrich Hegel, *Lectures on the History of Philosophy, 1825–6*, trans. Robert F. Brown and J. M. Stewart, ed. Robert F. Brown (Oxford: Oxford University Press, 2009), vol. 1, 208f. The question concerning the appropriation of Hegel's imbrication of inheritance and labor by Marxian materialism is pursued by Stefan Willer, "Kulturelles Erbe. Tradieren und Konservieren in der Moderne," in *Erbe. Übertragungskonzepte zwischen Natur und Kultur*, eds. Stefan Willer, Sigrid Weigel, and Bernhard Jussen (Berlin: Suhrkamp, 2013), 160–201, here 165–71.

32. Jacques Derrida, *Specters of Marx: The State of the Debt, the Work of Mourning, and the New International*, trans. Peggy Kamuf (New York: Routledge, 1994), 16.

34. Friedrich Nietzsche, *Also sprach Zarathustra, Kritische Studienausgabe*, eds. Giorgio Colli and Mazzino Montinari (Munich and Berlin: DTV and DeGruyter, 1999), vol. 4, 100, 94; *Thus Spoke Zarathustra*, trans. Adrian Del Caro, eds. Adrian Del Caro and Robert Pippin (Cambridge:

Cambridge University Press, 2006), 58, 54. An earlier version of part of this thesis appeared in my *Inheriting Walter Benjamin* and, in German, in *Verwaiste Hinterlassenschaften*.

35. Franz Kafka, *Der Proceß, Kritische Ausgabe*, ed. Malcolm Pasley (Frankfurt am Main: Fischer, 2002), 297.

36. William Faulkner, *Requiem for a Nun* (New York: Vintage, 2012), 73.

39. Jacques Derrida, *Positions*, trans. Alan Bass (Chicago: University of Chicago Press, 1981), 71.

41. Friedrich Nietzsche, *Der Antichrist, Kritische Studienausgabe*, eds. Giorgio Colli and Mazzino Montinari (Munich and Berlin: DTV and DeGruyter, 1999), vol. 6, 167.

42. Charlotte Brontë, *Jane Eyre* (New York: Vintage, 2009), 190.

44. Roland Barthes, "Myth Today," *Mythologies*, trans. Annette Lavers (New York: Noonday, 1988), 109–59, here 142. Anselm Kiefer, *Über Räume und Völker*, ed. Klaus Gallwitz (Frankfurt am Main: Suhrkamp, 1990), 166. Anselm Kiefer, Joseph Beuys, Jannis Kounellis, and Enzo Cucci, *Ein Gespräch/Una Discussione*, ed. Jacqueline Burckhardt (Zurich: Parkett, 1986), 19. An earlier version of part of this thesis appeared in my "History's Flight, Anselm Kiefer's Angels," *Connecticut Review*, 24:1 (spring 2002), 113–36, which I self-inherit here.

45. Søren Kierkegaard, *Diary of Søren Kierkegaard*, trans. Gerda Anderson, ed. Peter Rohde (New York: Philosophical Library, 1960), 111.

46. Immanuel Kant, *Kritik der Urteilskraft, Werkausgabe*, ed. Wilhelm Weischedel (Frankfurt am Main: Suhrkamp, 1974), vol. 10, 213. An earlier version of the sentences that comprise this thesis appeared in my *Afterness: Figures of Following in Modern Thought and Aesthetics* (New York: Columbia University Press, 2011).

48. Samuel Beckett, *Endgame*, in *The Grove Centenary Editions of Samual Beckett, Vol. 3: Dramatic Works*, ed. Paul Auster (New York: Grove, 2006), 100.

49. Jean-François Lyotard, "Foreword: After the Words," in Joseph Kosuth, *Art After Philosophy and After: Collected Writings, 1966–1990*, ed. Gabriele Guercio (Cambridge, MA: MIT Press, 1991), xv–xviii, here xv.

50. Martin Heidegger, "What Calls for Thinking?," trans. Fred D. Wieck and J. Glenn Gray, in *Basic Writings*, ed. David Farrell Krell (San Francisco: Harper, 1993), 365–91, here 380.

51. Jacques Derrida, "Mochlos, or The Conflict of the Faculties," trans. Richard Rand and Amy Wygant, *Eyes of the University: Right to Philosophy 2*, trans. Jan Plug and others (Stanford: Stanford University Press, 2004), 83–112, here 101.

52. Jacques Rancière, *The Ignorant Schoolmaster: Five Lessons in Intellectual*

Emancipation, trans. Kristin Ross (Stanford: Stanford University Press, 1991), 6f.

53. Stanley Cavell, *Little Did I Know: Excerpts from Memory* (Stanford: Stanford University Press, 2010), 446.

55. Heraclitus, *Fragments*, trans. and ed. Thomas M. Robinson (Toronto: University of Toronto Press, 1987), 44, 53.

57. Jacques Derrida and Elisabeth Roudinesco, "Choosing One's Heritage," in *For What Tomorrow . . . A Dialogue*, trans. Jeff Fort (Stanford: Stanford University Press, 2004), 1–19, here 3.

58. Peter Sloterdijk, *Polyloquien. Ein Sloterdijk Brevier* (Berlin: Suhrkamp, 2018), 77.

59. Roland Barthes, *The Fashion System*, trans. Matthew Ward and Richard Howard (Berkeley: University of California Press, 1990), 273.

60. Paul de Man, "Literary History and Literary Modernity," in *Blindness and Insight: Essays in the Rhetoric of Contemporary Criticism*, 2nd, rev. edn (Minneapolis: University of Minnesota Press, 1983), 142–65, here 148.

61. Maurice Blanchot, *The Writing of the Disaster*, trans. Ann Smock (Lincoln: University of Nebraska Press, 1995), 42.

62. Miguel de Cervantes, *Don Quixote*, trans. Peter Motteux, ed. John G. Lockhart (Boston, MA: Little, Brown, and Co., 1854), vol. 4, 377.

66. Walter Benjamin, *The Correspondence of Walter Benjamin, 1910–1940*, trans. Manfred R. Jacobson and Evelyn M. Jacobson, eds. Gershom Scholem and Theodor W. Adorno (Chicago: University of Chicago Press, 1994), 149.

67. Jacques Derrida, *Learning to Live Finally: The Last Interview*, trans. Pascale-Anne Brault and Michael Naas (Hoboken: Melville House, 2007), 33f.

69. William Faulkner, "The Art of Fiction," in *The Paris Review Interviews*, ed. Philip Gourevitch (New York: Picador, 2007), vol. 2, 34–57, here 54.

70. Walter Benjamin, "'The Regression of Poetry', by Carl Gustav Jochmann," trans. Edmund Jephcott, in *Walter Benjamin: Selected Writings, Vol. 4: 1938–1940*, eds. Michael W. Jennings and Howard Eiland (Cambridge, MA: Harvard University Press, 2003), 356–80, here 356.

71. Jean-Luc Nancy quoted in Simon Sparks, "Editor's Preface," in *Retreating the Political*, by Phillippe Lacoue-Labarthe and Jean-Luc Nancy, ed. Simon Sparks (London: Routledge, 1997), ix–xii, here xii.

72. Jean-Luc Nancy, "'What Is to Be Done?'," trans. Leslie Hill, in *Retreating the Political*, by Phillippe Lacoue-Labarthe and Jean-Luc Nancy, ed. Simon Sparks (London: Routledge, 1997), 157–8, here 158.

74. Stephen Greenblatt, *Shakespearean Negotiations: The Circulation of Social Energy in Renaissance England* (Berkeley: University of California Press, 1988), 1f.

76. Julian Barnes, *Nothing To Be Frightened Of* (New York: Knopf, 2008), 8.

77. Richard Pogue Harrison, *The Dominion of the Dead* (Chicago: University of Chicago Press, 2003), ix–x. An earlier version of the sentences included in this thesis appeared in my *Thinking With Adorno: The Uncoercive Gaze* (New York: Fordham University Press, 2019).

78. Hayden White and Robert Pogue Harrison, "We're Here to Discuss the Meaning of Life," *Chronicle of Higher Education*, website, published April 3, 2019. Last accessed January 8, 2020. URL <https://www.chronicle.com/article/We-re-Here-to-Discuss-the/246047>.

79. Michel Foucault, "What Is an Author?," trans. Josué V. Harari, *The Foucault Reader*, ed. Paul Rabinow (New York: Pantheon, 1984), 101–20, here 120.

80. Isaac Newton cited in Robert K. Merton, *On the Shoulders of Giants: A Shandean Postscript*, with a Foreword by Umberto Eco and an Afterword by Denis Donoghue (Chicago: University of Chicago Press, 1993), 1. Friedrich Nietzsche, *Also sprach Zarathustra, Kritische Studienausgabe*, eds. Giorgio Colli and Mazzino Montinari (Munich and Berlin: DTV and DeGruyter, 1999), vol. 4, 198.

83. Jacques Derrida, *Specters of Marx: The State of the Debt, the Work of Mourning, and the New International*, trans. Peggy Kamuf (New York: Routledge, 1994), 54, 21, 35, 91f. I borrow the substance of this thesis from my "The Debt of Inheritance Revisited: Heidegger's Mortgage, Derrida's Appraisal," *Oxford Literary Review*, 37:1 (2015), 67–91.

84. Walter Benjamin, "Über das mimetische Vermögen," *Gesammelte Schriften*, eds. Rolf Tiedemann and Hermann Schweppenhäuser (Frankfurt am Main: Suhrkamp, 1991), vol. 2, 210–13, here 213.

85. Katie Paterson, *Future Library*, Website, last accessed January 8, 2020. URL <https://www.futurelibrary.no>.

86. Jacques Derrida, *The Beast and the Sovereign II*, trans. Geoffrey Bennington, eds. Michel Lisse, Marie-Louise Mallet, and Ginette Michaud (Chicago: University of Chicago Press, 2011), 132, 130.

87. Alois Riegl, "Der moderne Denkmalskultus. Sein Wesen und seine Geschichte," in *Gesammelte Aufsätze*, with an Afterword by Wolfgang Kemp (Berlin: Mann, 1995), 144–93, here 144. Robert Musil, *Nachlaß zu Lebzeiten* (Stuttgart: Reclam, 2013), 57.

89. Karl Marx, "For a Ruthless Criticism of Everything Existing," trans. Ronald Rogowski, in *The Marx–Engels Reader*, ed. Robert C. Tucker (New York: Norton, 1978), 12–15, here 13.

90. Karl Marx, *The Eighteenth Brumaire of Louis Bonaparte. The Karl Marx Library, Vol. I: On Revolution*, trans. and ed. Saul K. Padover (New York: McGraw Hill, 1972), 245. Previous versions of parts of this thesis appeared in my "Interpretation, Revolution, Inheritance: Benjamin with Marx," *MLN*, 133:3 (2018), 521–43.

91. Art Spiegelman, *MetaMaus: A Look Inside a Modern Classic, Maus* (New York: Pantheon, 2011), 155.

92. Friedrich Nietzsche, *The Antichrist, The Portable Nietzsche*, trans. and ed. Walter Kaufmann (New York: Penguin, 1982), 565–656, here 650.

93. Ralph Waldo Emerson, *The Conduct of Life: Essays and Lectures* (New York: Library of America, 1983), 937–1124, here 1019f.

94. Jacques Derrida, *The Animal That Therefore I Am*, trans. David Wills, ed. Marie-Louise Mallet (New York: Fordham University Press, 2008), 3, 11.

96. Brecht cited in Jan Knopf, "Bertolt Brecht," in *Metzler Autoren Lexikon*, ed. Bernd Lutz (Stuttgart: Metzler, 1997), 92–6, here 96.

97. Franz Kafka, *Nachgelassene Schriften und Fragmente II, Kritische Ausgabe*, ed. Jost Schillemeit (Frankfurt am Main: Fischer, 1992), 90.

98. Mahatma Gandhi cited in Vinay Lal, "Gandhi's West, the West's Gandhi," *New Literary History*, 40:2 (2009), 283–313, here 283. As Lal also discusses, the precise wording of Gandhi's response may be partially apocryphal.

100. Emily Dickinson, *Selected Letters*, ed. Thomas H. Johnson (Cambridge, MA: Harvard University Press, 1986), 412; cited in Seth Lerer, *Tradition: A Feeling for the Literary Past* (Oxford: Oxford University Press, 2016), viii.

101. Hubert Dreyfus, "Heidegger on the Connection Between Nihilism, Art, Technology, and Politics," in *The Cambridge Companion to Heidegger*, 2nd edn, ed. Charles Guignon (Cambridge: Cambridge University Press, 2006), 345–72, here 351. I borrow the sentences of this thesis from a footnote in my *Inheriting Walter Benjamin*, where they appear in an earlier version.

104. Friedrich Nietzsche, *Ecce Homo: How One Becomes What One Is*, trans. R. J. Hollingdale (London: Penguin, 2004), 8, 4, 7. A few sentences of this thesis are borrowed from my essay "Troubled Origins: Accounting for Oneself," forthcoming in *Derrida Today*.

105. Marguerite Duras, *Practicalities: Marguerite Duras Speaks to Jérôme Beaujour*, trans. Barbara Bray (New York: Grove, 1990), 46.

106. Franz Kafka, *Letters to Felice*, trans. James Stern and Elisabeth Duckworth, eds. Erich Heller and Jürgen Born (New York: Schocken, 1973), 272.

107. Franz Kafka, "The Worry of the Father of the Family," in *Kafka's Selected Stories*, trans. and ed. Stanley Corngold (New York: Norton, 2007), 72–3, here 73.

108. Joan Copjec, "The Inheritance of Potentiality: An Interview with Joan Copjec," *E-rea* Website, published December 15, 2014. Last accessed January 8, 2020. URL <http://journals.openedition.org/erea/4102>.

109. Christa Wolf, *Sommerstück*, in *Werke* (Munich: Luchterhand, 2001), vol. 10, 11.

110. Martin Walser, *A Gushing Fountain*, trans. David Dollenmayer (New York: Arcade Publishing, 2015), 3.

111. Jacques Derrida, "As If I Were Dead: An Interview with Jacques Derrida," in *Applying: To Derrida*, eds. John Brannigan, Ruth Robbins, and Julian Wolfreys (New York: St. Martin's, 1996), 212–26, here 216f.

112. Johann Wolfgang Goethe, *Maxims and Reflections*, trans. Elisabeth Stopp (London: Penguin, 1998), 128.

113. Walter Benjamin, "Nietzsche und das Archiv seiner Schwester," in *Gesammelte Schriften*, eds. Rolf Tiedemann and Hermann Schweppenhäuser (Frankfurt am Main: Suhrkamp, 1991), vol. 3, 323-6, here 326. Walter Benjamin, *Gesammelte Briefe*, eds. Christoph Gödde and Henri Lonitz (Frankfurt am Main: Surhkamp, 1996), vol. 2, 392. An earlier version of the sentences in this thesis appeared in my essay "Interpretation, revolution, inheritance: Benjamin with Marx," *MLN*, 133:3 (2018), 521–43.

115. David Carr, "Husserl's Problematic Concept of the Life-World," *American Philosophical Quarterly*, 7:4 (October 1970), 331–9, here 331.

116. Albert Einstein, "The Heirs of the Ages," in *The World As I See It*, trans. Alan Harris (New York: Covici Friede, 1934), 234.

117. Michel Foucault, *The History of Sexuality, Volume I: An Introduction*, trans. Robert Hurley (New York: Vintage, 1990), 27.

118. Bertolt Brecht, "An die Nachgeborenen/To Those Born Later," in *Poetry and Prose*, eds. Reinhold Grimm and Carolina Molina y Vedia (New York: Continuum, 2003), 70–5, here 71. Giorgio Agamben, *Remnants of Auschwitz: The Witness and the Archive*, trans. Daniel Heller-Roazen (New York: Zone Books, 2002), 32f. Karl Marx, "Theses on Feuerbach," in *The Marx–Engels Reader*, ed. Robert C. Tucker (New York: Norton, 1978), 143–5, here 145. Paul Celan, "A LEAF, treeless," in *Breathturn to Timestead: The Collected Later Poetry*, trans. Pierre Joris (New York: Farrar Straus Giroux, 2014), 369. A German version of part of this thesis appeared in the chapter "Die kritische Theorie erben? Ein Gespräch über Bäume heute," in *Verwaiste Hinterlassenschaften*; the version included here is based on a translation by Kristina Mendicino.

120. Sigmund Freud, *Civilization and Its Discontents*, trans. James Strachey (New York: Norton, 1989), 112.

122. Peter Handke, *The Weight of the World*, trans. Ralph Manheim (New York: Farrar, Straus & Giroux, 1984), 7.

123. Hannah Arendt, "Martin Heidegger at Eighty," trans. Alfred Hofstadter, in *Heidegger and Modern Philosophy: Critical Essays*, ed. Michael Murray (New Haven: Yale University Press, 1978), 293–303, here 294.

124. Judith Schalansky, *Verzeichnis einiger Verluste* (Berlin: Suhrkamp, 2018), 16, 17, 19.

125. Bruno Bosteels, "Can Change Be Thought? A Dialogue with Alain Badiou," in *Alain Badiou: Philosophy and Its Conditions*, ed. Gabriel Riera (Albany: State University of New York Press, 2005), 237–62, here 238.

126. Karl Ove Knausgaard, *Winter*, trans. Ingvild Burkey (New York: Penguin, 2018), 236f.

127. Fredric Jameson, *Postmodernism, or, The Cultural Logic of Late Capitalism* (Durham: Duke University Press, 1991), 15f.

128. Reinhard Lettau, interviewed by journalist Cornelia Geißer, in "Auf einmal ist der Feind weg. Der Schriftsteller Reinhard Lettau über Berlin, den PEN und das Klima im Lande," *Berliner Zeitung*, February 24, 1995. Last accessed through the web archive of *Berliner Zeitung* on January 9, 2020. URL <https://archiv.berliner-zeitung.de/der-schriftsteller-reinhard-lettau-ueber-berlin--den-pen-und-das-klima-im-lande-auf-einmal-ist-der-feind-weg-17558954>.

131. John Sallis, *Stone* (Bloomington: Indiana University Press, 1994), 45.

133. Elias Canetti, *Aufzeichnungen, 1942–1948* (Munich: DTV, 1969), 13.

134. Gilles Deleuze, "What Is the Creative Act?," in *Two Regimes of Madness: Texts and Interviews 1975–1995*, trans. Ames Hodges and Mike Taormina, ed. David Lapoujade (New York: Semiotext(e), 2006), 312–24, here 313.

135. Botho Strauß, *Allein mit allen. Gedankenbuch*, ed. Sebastian Kleinschmidt (Munich: Hanser, 2014), 250.

137. Rux Martin, "Truth, Power, Self: An Interview with Michel Foucault, October 25, 1982," in *Technologies of the Self. A Seminar with Michael Foucault*, eds. Luther H. Martin, Huck Gutman, and Patrick H. Hutton (Amherst: University of Massachusetts Press, 1988), 9–15, here 9.

138. Michel de Montaigne, "Of the Inconsistency of Our Actions," in *Montaigne's Essays and Selected Writings: A Bilingual Edition*, trans. and ed. Donald M. Frame (New York: St. Martin's, 1963), 143–62, here 155.

142. Bertolt Brecht, *Die Dreigroschenoper*, in *Die Stücke von Bertolt Brecht in einem Band* (Frankfurt am Main: Suhrkamp, 1987), 165–202, here 186.

144. *Marx zum Vergnügen*, ed. Bert Sander (Stuttgart: Reclam, 2012), 175f.

145. Benedict Anderson, *Imagined Communities: Reflections on the Origins and Spread of Nationalism*, revised edn (London: Verso, 1991), 187.

146. Richard Ellmann, *James Joyce*, new and revised edn (Oxford: Oxford University Press, 1983), 397.

147. David Farrell Krell, "Creative Solitudes," in *The Philosophy of Creative Solitudes*, ed. David Jones (London: Bloomsbury, 2019), 21–37, here 22f.

148. Elias Canetti, *The Secret Heart of the Clock: Notes, Aphorisms, Fragments 1973–1985*, trans. Joel Agee (New York: Farrar, Straus & Giroux, 1989), 79.